The
WISCONSIN
Journey

The WISCONSIN Journey

Kurt Leichtle

with Susan Myers and Aimee Larsen Stoddard

GIBBS·SMITH
P
PUBLISHER

SALT LAKE CITY

2008   2007   2006   2005   2004   2003   10   9   8   7   6   5

Copyright © 2002 by Gibbs Smith, Publisher
Second Edition © 2003

Gibbs Smith, Publisher
P.O. Box 667
Layton, UT 84041

(800) 748-5439
text@gibbs-smith.com
www.gibbs-smith.com/textbooks

Editors: Susan A. Myers, Aimee Larsen Stoddard

Associate editors: Courtney Johnson Thomas, Anne Robbins

Book design: Kathleen Timmerman

Cover photo: John Ivanko

Other photograph and art credits appear at the end of the book.

Printed and bound in China

About the Authors:

Kurt Leichtle is a professor of Wisconsin and U.S. history at the University of Wisconsin-River Falls, where he also advises student teachers. He received his Ph.D. and MA degrees from the University of Illinois at Chicago.

Susan A. Myers has a bachelor's degree from Brigham Young University and has completed graduate work in education, English, and art. She works with history and reading specialists as an author and editor and has published fifteen quality history textbooks for children.

Aimee Larsen Stoddard has a degree from Weber State University in English and history. She has edited numerous textbooks and university literary journals.

ISBN 1-58685-061-X

To Karen, Kyle, and Kee

Contents

Maps

Wisconsin's State Symbols

Animal: Badger

Bird: Robin

Insect: Honeybee

Fish: Muskie

Tree: Sugar Maple

Dog: American Water Spaniel

Flower: Wood Violet

Domestic Animal: Dairy Cow

Wild Animal: White-tailed Deer

2

Chapter 1

PLACES TO LOCATE

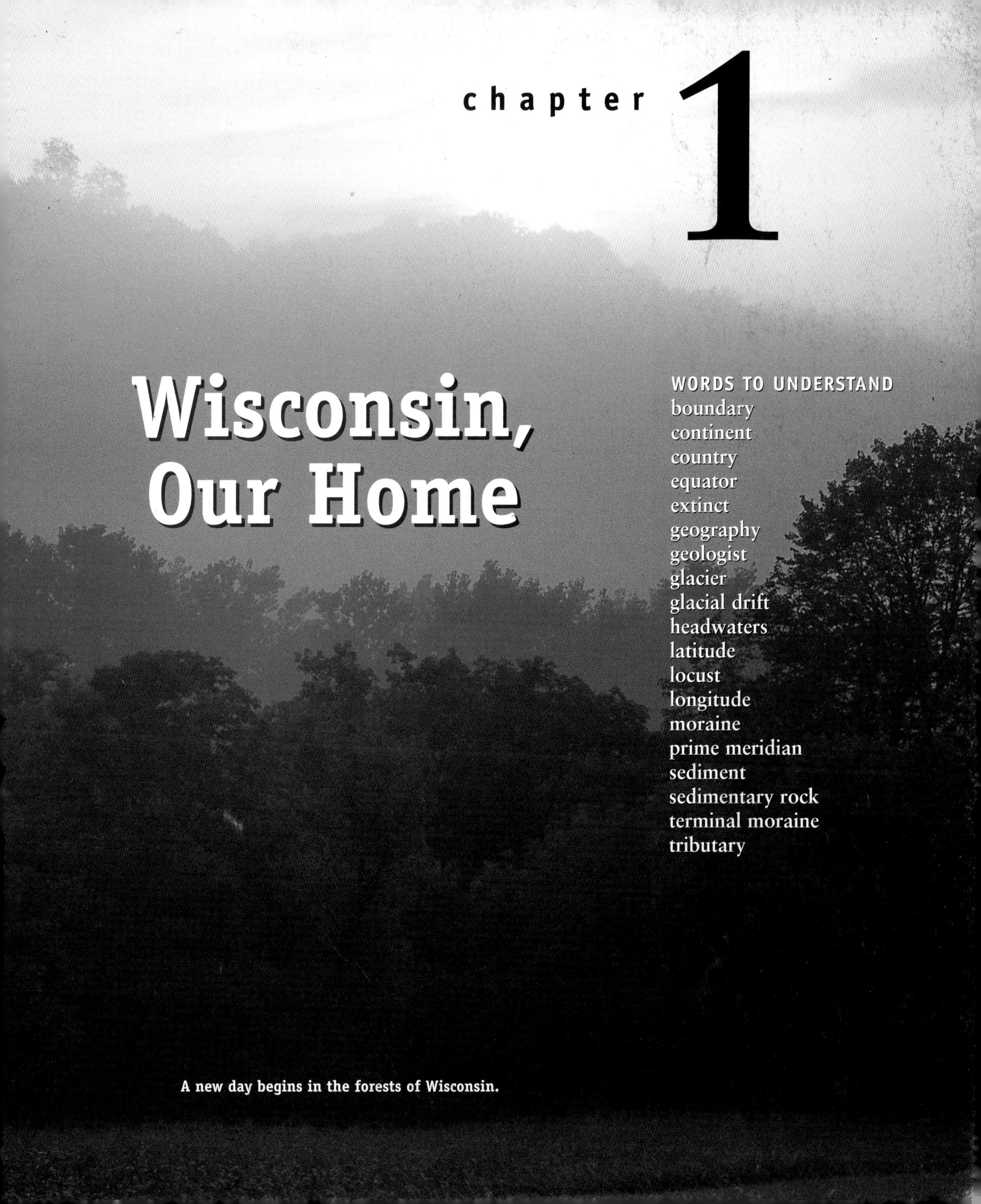

chapter 1

Wisconsin, Our Home

WORDS TO UNDERSTAND

boundary
continent
country
equator
extinct
geography
geologist
glacier
glacial drift
headwaters
latitude
locust
longitude
moraine
prime meridian
sediment
sedimentary rock
terminal moraine
tributary

A new day begins in the forests of Wisconsin.

4

PLACES TO LOCATE
North America
Canada
United States of America
Mexico
Wisconsin
Illinois
Michigan
Minnesota
Iowa
Great Lakes
Lake Superior
Lake Michigan
Lake Winnebago
St. Croix River
Fox River
Wisconsin River
Mississippi River
Gulf of Mexico

WORDS TO UNDERSTAND
boundary
continent
country
equator
geography
headwaters
latitude
longitude
prime meridian
tributary

The Land We Call Home

Wisconsin seems very large. Yet it is just one small part of the world. Because we live in Wisconsin, it is important to us. It is our home. Millions of people all over the world live in places that are important to them.

In this chapter, we will learn about Wisconsin by studying its *geography*. Geography is the study of the land, water, plants, animals, and people of a place. First we will learn where Wisconsin is located in the world. We will learn what the land is like and how it got that way. We will see how people use the land and take care of the land. We will see how people in Wisconsin are connected with people all over the world.

Where Do You Live?

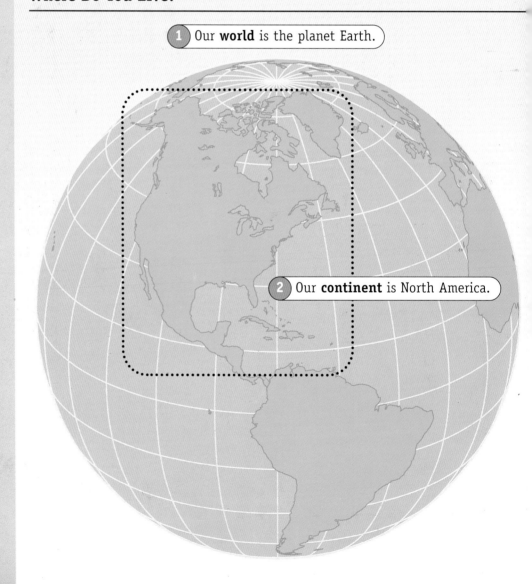

1 Our **world** is the planet Earth.

2 Our **continent** is North America.

Why is it important to know about the geography of a place? Geography affects where we live. It affects how we live.

Where in the World Are We?

We all know we live on planet Earth. But just where on earth do we live? Wisconsin is located on one of the world's *continents*. Continents are very large land areas. They have oceans on many sides. Wisconsin is on the continent of North America.

Wisconsin is part of a *country* in North America. A country is a land region under the control of one government. Our country is the United States of America. Canada is a country to the north of us. Mexico is a country to the south of us.

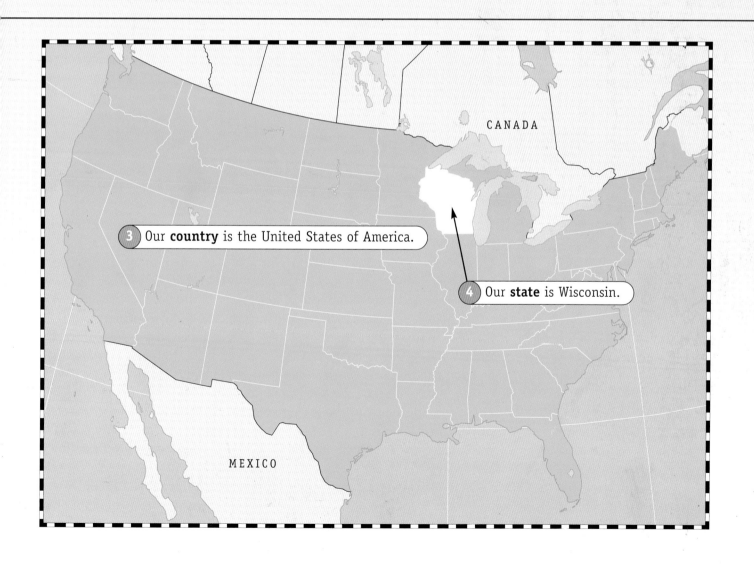

3 Our **country** is the United States of America.

4 Our **state** is Wisconsin.

CANADA

MEXICO

Water, Water, Everywhere

The name Wisconsin comes from an Indian word that means "where the waters gather."

This is the headwater of the Wisconsin River near the Michigan border.

▲ Photo by Wisconsin Division of Tourism

The sun sets over the Wisconsin River. There are forty-seven dams on the river, but laws say that part of the river must stay in its natural state. No dams can be built there.

Our state has water on three of its four sides. There are also more than 10,000 streams and 8,700 lakes.

Rivers often start in higher land. They are just small streams of melted snow. The starting place for a river is called its **headwaters**.

The streams join other streams and flow into a lake or larger river. As a river flows to the ocean, other rivers called **tributaries** flow into it. The river becomes wider with all the new water.

The many waterways in Wisconsin are important transportation routes. In the past, Native Americans, explorers, and pioneers used the waterways like we use highways today. It was easier and faster to travel on water than on land. The land was covered with many trees and rocks.

The people crossed Lake Michigan in boats and paddled up the Fox River. They crossed Lake Winnebago and some smaller lakes. Then the travelers carried their canoes across the narrow stretch of land that was between the Fox and the Wisconsin Rivers. They paddled down the Wisconsin River all the way to the Mississippi River.

On the Mississippi, travelers could float all the way to the Gulf of Mexico and out to the ocean. By land, this trip would have been almost impossible. It would have taken a very long time.

▲ Photo by John D. Ivanko

Everyone Needs Water

Everyone needs water. People have always built their villages or towns near rivers and lakes. Today, water comes to our homes in pipes under the ground. Rivers and lakes are still important. Ships transport goods back and forth to people in many cities. Water gives beauty to the land.

Do you like to fish, swim, and water ski? Do you like to wade along the beach?

A Home for Fish

Lakes and rivers are important sources of food. Even families far away from lakes eat fresh fish, frozen fish, and canned fish. Not all the animals in the lakes, rivers, and streams are fish. Animals that have shells, such as oysters, are shellfish. They have hard shells on the outside instead of bones on the inside. Oysters live in the Mississippi River.

People fish on the Great Lakes for fun. They also make money catching and selling fish.

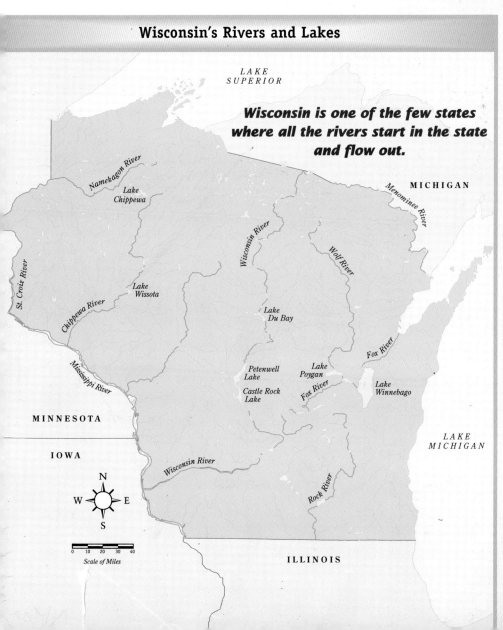

Wisconsin's Rivers and Lakes

Wisconsin is one of the few states where all the rivers start in the state and flow out.

LAKE SUPERIOR

MICHIGAN

Namekagon River

Lake Chippewa

Menominee River

Wisconsin River

Wolf River

St. Croix River

Chippewa River

Lake Wissota

Lake Du Bay

Fox River

Mississippi River

Petenwell Lake

Lake Poygan

Fox River

Castle Rock Lake

Lake Winnebago

MINNESOTA

LAKE MICHIGAN

IOWA

Wisconsin River

Rock River

N
W E
S

ILLINOIS

0 10 20 30 40
Scale of Miles

One of the most beautiful places on the Wisconsin River is called the Dells. A dell is a narrow valley. Swiftly flowing water has carved strange-looking rocks in the Dells.

A Winnebago Indian legend says the Dells were formed by a snake that forced its body through solid rock.

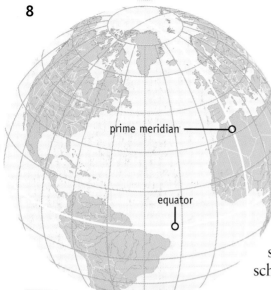

prime meridian

equator

Exact location is the exact position of a place. Every place in the world has an exact location that is measured by *longitude* and *latitude* lines. You can see these imaginary lines on a map or a globe. Most of the time, however, we use an address to give us an exact location. You might say, "I live at 405 Washington Street, Madison, Wisconsin." This tells your friend *exactly* where to find your house.

Relative location describes where something is in relation to other things. For example, Wisconsin is *next* to the states of Minnesota, Michigan, Illinois, and Iowa. Wisconsin touches Lake Superior and Lake Michigan. You could also tell someone that you live near the Wisconsin River, or next to the school, or down the hall from your friend's apartment.

Drawing Lines Around the World

Most maps have lines that run side to side and up and down. These are latitude and longitude lines. They run all the way around the world. Latitude lines run east and west (side to side). Longitude lines run north and south (up and down).

Along the lines you will find numbers. These are the exact latitude and longitude numbers. Each number has a tiny circle by it. This is a symbol for a degree. A degree is part of a circle or globe.

The numbers tell exactly how far north of the **equator** Wisconsin is. They tell how far west of the **prime meridian** Wisconsin is. You can see the equator and prime meridian on the globe at the top of the page.

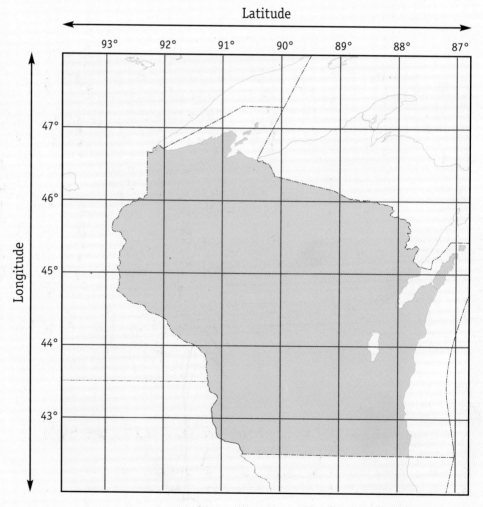

Activity

We're Surrounded!

The land is natural. It has always been here. But people divide up the land. They decide where *boundaries*—the outside edges—should be. They make maps to show the boundaries.

How do people decide where the boundaries should be? Look at a map of the Midwest and find Wisconsin. What natural features are used as boundaries? Natural features include rivers, lakes, and mountains.

1. Are any of Wisconsin's boundaries rivers? What are they?
2. Are any of Wisconsin's boundaries lakes? What are they?
3. Are any of the boundaries imaginary lines? These are boundaries made by people. Sometimes they follow latitude lines. Sometimes they follow old trails. Sometimes they are chosen for other reasons.

Have you ever seen the beautiful wide Mississippi River?
It forms much of our western boundary.

▼ Photo by John D. Ivanko

Lesson 1 Memory Master

1. What do we call the study of the location, land, water, plants, animals, and people of a place?
2. What continent, country, and state do you live in?
3. What do we call the place where a river starts?
4. Name the states, rivers, and lakes that form Wisconsin's boundaries.

Lesson **2**

Ancient Times

PLACES TO LOCATE
North America
Polar Region
Canada
Wisconsin
Great Lakes

WORDS TO UNDERSTAND
extinct
geologist
glacier
glacial drift
locust
moraine
sediment
sedimentary rock
terminal moraine

Ancient Rocks and Seas

Geologists are scientists who study layers of rock to learn more about the past. They study how water, wind, and temperature have changed the rock. Geologists have learned that long ago our land was different from what it is now.

When geologists find seashells in a layer of rock, they know that large seas once covered that land. Most of Wisconsin was covered by water at one time. The sea was filled with small and large animals. Even crocodiles swam here!

Large animals lived in the ancient seas.

After the seas went away the land was like a tropical forest. Ferns grew as high as trees. Large dragonflies flew in the air.

The bottom of the sea was covered with *sediment*. The sediment was made of gravel, sand, mud, and shells of tiny sea animals. Later, the sediment was pressed into stone by the weight of the heavy earth above it. *Sedimentary rock* was formed.

One kind of sedimentary rock comes from layers of fine sand that were pressed together for many years. Can you guess what this rock is called? It is called sandstone. There is a lot of sandstone in our state.

After many years, the great seas finally went away. The land was more like a wet forest than the Wisconsin we know today. Ferns grew higher than most trees you have seen. *Locusts* buzzed in the trees. They were like large grasshoppers. Dragonflies with wingspans of more than two feet glided through the forest.

Sedimentary rock was formed by layers of sand, shells, and rocks.

The Ice Age

Long before any people lived where you live now, a sheet of ice formed in northern Canada. As the air got colder and colder, the ice got thicker. In some places, it was over a mile thick. The weight of the *glaciers* caused them to move slowly over the land.

Glaciers moved over Canada. Then they crept slowly over the northern places of what is now the United States.

During the Ice Age, summer never came. It never got warm enough to melt the ice. Plants were buried under ice. Animals died or moved farther south where it was warmer.

Mountains and hard rocks such as granite slowed the moving glaciers. The ice moved faster through the valleys. The moving ice smoothed out the land like sandpaper smooths rough wood.

The glaciers came part way across what is now Wisconsin. Then the air got warmer and the ice started to melt. The places that were never touched by glaciers have many more steep hills than the rest of Wisconsin.

About a million years ago, glaciers covered part of our state.

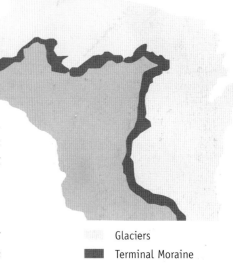

▨ Glaciers
▰ Terminal Moraine

New Soil and New Hills

Moving glaciers from the north carried huge boulders, smaller rocks, and soil. The soil and rocks brought from other places are called *glacial drift*. Glacial drift was left behind when the ice melted.

Over and over again, the glaciers melted and then came back. Each time they brought more soil.

As they moved, glaciers also pushed mounds of earth in front of them. What happened to all that earth and rock? The melted ice left a high wormlike ridge. Some mounds were so high they look like long hills or ridges today. This land is called a *terminal moraine*. Terminal means "the end."

A *moraine* is a large amount of dirt and rock left by a glacier.

The glaciers left another mark on our landscape. In one place, large blocks of ice were buried in the glacial drift. Years later, when the air warmed up and the ice melted, the earth on top fell in. The land was dotted with these deep holes. Water often filled the deeper holes. We call these kettle moraines. They are like kettles filled with water. Today, they look like ponds.

New Lakes and Rivers

Sometimes the glaciers carved out deep ridges and wide valleys. These low places filled with water. The Great Lakes were formed this way.

The moraines made natural dams that stopped rivers from flowing. The trapped water formed new lakes. As the lakes filled with more and more water, the water flowed over the earth dams and made new paths to the ocean. The water formed new rivers. In some places, the water just spread out over the low land. The land became a wet and swampy marsh.

Ice Age Animals

A little over a hundred years ago, a skeleton was found in Wisconsin. The mastodon skeleton was nearly eleven feet high. This is as tall as three fourth-grade students standing on each other's heads.

In 1999, a three-year-old boy and his cousins saw a bone sticking out of the ground. His mother found out from scientists at the university that it was part of a woolly mammoth. Parts of twenty mammoth skeletons have been found in Wisconsin. Scientists believe there are many more under the ground.

Woolly mammoths had curved tusks sixteen feet long. They had long shaggy fur that hung almost to the ground. Strands of fur were three feet long. The animals ate hundreds of pounds of grass each day. They lived to be sixty years old.

Deer, caribou, giant camels, huge bison, and small horses ate green grasses and leaves. These same animals were then hunted and eaten by tigers. After the Ice Age, men also hunted the animals. The hunters used spears with sharp stone points.

As the weather got warmer and warmer, many kinds of animals became *extinct*. They no longer live on the earth.

Mammoths and mastodons were some of the largest Ice Age animals.

The saber-toothed cat hunted other animals.

Fossils

Fossils are prints or remains of plants or animals in rock. When scientists study fossils, they learn about life long ago. The state fossil is a trilobite.

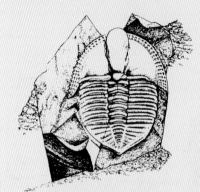

Small trilobite fossils are found in many places.

Shells from ancient seas are found in rock.

Lesson 2 Memory Master

1. Geologists study _____ to learn about the past.
2. How do we know that Wisconsin used to be covered by large seas?
3. In what ways did glaciers change the land?
4. What are some Ice Age animals?

What's the point?

It's exciting to know that we are part of a state, a continent, and a planet! The more we know about our state, the more interested we'll be when we drive over a bridge across the Mississippi River, camp in the woods, or visit a large city.

The view outside your window would have been very different a million years ago. That was the Ice Age. The ice is gone now. Moving glaciers smoothed out much of our land. In other places, they left behind high hills. We are surrounded by land carved by glaciers.

Paul Bunyan and the Great Lakes

You just learned that Ice Age glaciers formed the Great Lakes. But have you ever heard the story of Paul Bunyan, the giant woodsman?

Paul Bunyan stories are folk tales. Some parts of a folk tale are just made up. They are not true.

Paul Bunyan, so the tale goes, was born in Maine. He was so big that he slept in a cradle floating in the ocean. When he grew up, Paul decided the East was too crowded. He headed to the Midwest to work in the lumber camps.

Paul's best friend Babe, a blue ox, came with him. If a road was too crooked, Paul just hitched Babe to the road and pulled it straight.

On the way to Wisconsin, Paul and Babe walked through a marshy place. Their very large footprints left deep holes in the ground.

Then, in just a few giant steps, Paul climbed to the top of a mountain. Wanting a little fun, he jumped into the Wisconsin River below. The great splash scattered water all over. The water filled up the footprints and made the Great Lakes. The great splash made lots of smaller lakes, too.

One day Paul was floating logs down the Wisconsin River. He saw them all jammed up. Nothing would move. The logjam was 200 feet high. The jam was too big for even Paul and his crew to break up.

Paul called Babe over and started to tickle him with a pine tree. Babe thought that a bunch of flies were bothering him. He swished his tail to chase them away. The wind was so strong that soon the river started flowing backward. The logjam broke up.

When all the trees in Wisconsin had been cut down, Paul and Babe moved west. They worked in lumber camps in Minnesota, the Dakotas, and Montana. Those are adventure stories for another time.

Activity

Write a Fictional Story

Fiction is a story that is not true. The stories of Paul Bunyan are fiction. With a partner or small group, make up a fictional person. Think about how the person might have formed rivers, mountains, farmland, or other landforms you read about in this chapter. Think of a pet the person might have.

Describe the person in your story. How old is the person? What does the person look like? What makes the person interesting? What makes the pet fun to think about?

Use lots of action verbs as you write the story on paper. As you write, be sure to start each sentence with a capital letter. End each sentence with a period, question mark, or exclamation mark.

Chapter 1 Review

1. What is geography?

2. What word describes rivers that flow into a larger river?

3. Describe the relative location of your home. Give the exact location.

4. Give examples of two different kinds of boundaries.

5. Name the states, rivers, and lakes that surround Wisconsin.

6. Which scientists study layers of rock to learn about the past?

7. What is sedimentary rock made of?

8. Did glaciers cover the land where you live?

9. Name two ways that glaciers changed the land in Wisconsin.

10. Name two or more Ice Age animals.

11. What does it mean when an animal is extinct?

12. What is Wisconsin's state fossil?

Activity

Reading a Map

There are many kinds of maps. Can you think of some? Perhaps you first thought of a road map. You might use it on a vacation trip. Maps help us get to where we want to go. They show us where places are.

Most maps have symbols you need to know. Here are some of them:

Compass: Maps show the directions north, south, east, and west. Most maps have north at the top. It helps to read a map if you put the map so that you are facing north. Then west will be on your left and east will be on your right. Where will south be?

LEGEND
★ State Capital
● Major City
〜 River

Legend or Key: Mapmakers use symbols to stand for certain things such as rivers or cities. Whenever there are symbols, there is a key or legend that explains what the symbols mean. What do the symbols on this legend represent?

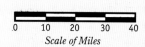

Scale of Miles

Scale of Miles: To show us distances, or how far apart places really are, mapmakers use a scale of miles. One inch on a map might mean 100 miles, 1,000 miles, or even more. About how many miles is it from Madison to Milwaukee? Which is the shorter distance: from Appleton to Oshkosh or from Beaver Dam to Sun Prairie?

Wisconsin

LAKE SUPERIOR

MICHIGAN

Superior

Washburn
Ashland
Hurley

Namekagon River

Hayward
Lake Chippewa

Grantsburg

Shell Lake

Eagle River   Florence

Menominee River

Phillips

Rhinelander

Balsam Lake

Ladysmith

Crandon

Wisconsin River

St. Croix River

Barron

Wolf River

Merrill

Antigo

Marinette

Medford

Wausau

Keshena

Oconto

Sturgeon Bay

Hudson

Menomonie

Lake Wissota

Chippewa Falls

Lake Du Bay

Shawano

River Falls

Chippewa River

Eau Claire

Ellsworth

Marshfield

Stevens Point

Green Bay
Kewaunee

Durand

Neillsville

Whitehall

Wisconsin Rapids

Waupaca

Appleton
Neenah   Menasha

Fox River

Alma

Black River Falls

Petenwell Lake

Lake Poygan

Two Rivers
Manitowoc

Mississippi River

Sparta

Castle Rock Lake

Wautoma

Fox River

Oshkosh

Chilton

Lake Winnebago

La Crosse

Adams

Green Lake

Montello

Fond Du Lac

Sheboygan

Mauston

Viroqua

Wisconsin Dells   Portage

MINNESOTA

IOWA

Baraboo

Beaver Dam

West Bend

LAKE MICHIGAN

Richland Center

Jeneau

Port Washington

Wisconsin River

Sun Prairie   Watertown

Prairie Du Chien

Madison ★

Milwaukee

Jefferson

Waukesha

Dodgeville

Rock River

Whitewater

Lancaster

Janesville   Elkhorn

Racine

Darlington

Monroe

Beloit

Kenosha

N
W   E
S

0 10 20 30 40
Scale of Miles

ILLINOIS

PLACES TO LOCATE
Canada
Wisconsin
Green Bay
Madison
Milwaukee
Chicago, Illinois
Great Lakes
Lake Superior
Lake Michigan
Lake Winnebago
Mississippi River
Apostle Islands
Door Peninsula
Horican Marsh

Our Beautiful State

Flat land and low rolling hills are good places for growing corn and other crops.
Photo by John D. Ivanko

chapter **2**

Lesson **1**

The Land

PLACES TO LOCATE
Green Bay
Madison
Milwaukee
Chicago, Illinois
Great Lakes
Lake Superior
Lake Michigan
Lake Winnebago
Mississippi River
Apostle Islands
Door Peninsula
Horican Marsh

WORDS TO UNDERSTAND
agriculture
landform
region

Landforms

Landforms are different shapes and formations of land and water. It is important to know about landforms because people use different landforms in different ways. Your life would be a little different, for instance, if you lived near Lake Michigan than if you lived in a forest far away from the lake.

How many of these landforms have you seen?

MOUNTAIN:
a very high land formation. Wisconsin doesn't have any tall mountains.

RIVER:
a natural stream of moving water. The Mississippi and St. Croix Rivers form one of our state borders.

LAKE:
a large body of water fed by streams and rivers. Lake Winnebago is our largest lake.

HARBOR:
a sheltered part of a body of water deep enough for anchoring ships. Superior and Milwaukee harbors are natural. Workers have dug the Racine and Kenosha harbors deeper.

PENINSULA:
land that has water on three sides. The "thumb" of land that starts at Green Bay and sticks out into Lake Michigan is called the Door Peninsula. Early travelers who came across the lake thought this place was the door into the land.

Land Regions

A *region* is another way to tell about a place. Geographers divide large areas of the world into smaller parts. We call these parts regions. Regions are places that are alike in some way. Land regions have common landforms, such as lakes, valleys, mountains, or hills.

A region can be as large as a continent or as small as your neighborhood. You can live in many regions at the same time. For example, you might live in a coastal region where ships move in and out and a farming region where corn and hay are grown.

That's Big!

Largest city: Milwaukee

Longest river: Wisconsin River

Largest inland lake: Winnebago

What do you think?

Why do you think people usually build cities on flat land near water? Think about industry, transportation, and things people need. Why do farmers grow crops on flat land instead of in the mountains?

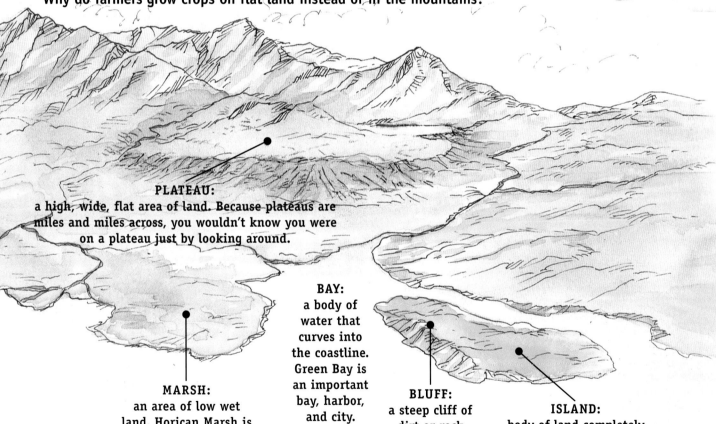

PLATEAU:
a high, wide, flat area of land. Because plateaus are miles and miles across, you wouldn't know you were on a plateau just by looking around.

MARSH:
an area of low wet land. Horican Marsh is home to many birds and water animals.

BAY:
a body of water that curves into the coastline. Green Bay is an important bay, harbor, and city.

BLUFF:
a steep cliff of dirt or rock above a river or lake. There are many bluffs along Lake Superior and the Mississippi River.

ISLAND:
body of land completely surrounded by water. The Apostle Islands are off Chemagenon Point on Lake Superior. Madeline Island can be reached by ferryboat in the summer and over the ice in the winter.

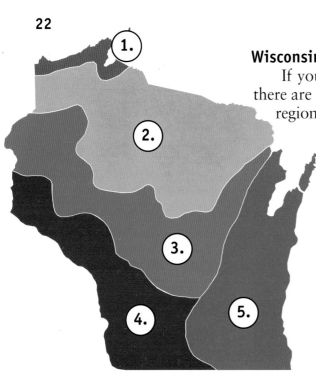

Wisconsin's Land Regions

If you were a bird flying over Wisconsin, you would see that there are five very different kinds of land in our state. The five land regions are:

1. **Lake Superior Lowlands**

2. **Northern Highland**

3. **Central Plain**

4. **Western Upland**

5. **Eastern Ridges and Lowlands**

Five Land Regions

1. Lake Superior Lowlands

The Lake Superior Lowlands are a strip of lakeshore in the northern part of Wisconsin. The region is cut by streams coming down from the highlands. The largest city in this region is Superior.

Ships unload their cargo at piers on Lake Superior.

2. Northern Highland

The highlands used to have tall mountains, but moving glaciers ground down the rocky peaks. The soil became sandy and rocky. It was just right for pine trees.

Millions of pine trees were cut into lumber to build the houses of the Midwest. Today, the hills are covered with forests. Hundreds of small lakes make the region a great place to camp, hike, and fish.

Camp with your family in the woods and enjoy nature.

3. Central Plain

The Central Plain curves around the center of the state. It has rich soil that makes it an ideal place for farming. Wisconsin's fame as a dairy state comes from the many dairy farms here.

▲ Farms grow food for all of us.

▼ Holstein cows provide rich milk.

▲ Photos by Wisconsin Division of Tourism

▲ Photo of cows by John D. Ivanko

The Midwest

A long time ago, most of the people in the United States lived along the coast of the Atlantic Ocean. To them, places as far away as the Mississippi River were called "the West." Places in between were called "the Midwest."

Today, the states around the Great Lakes are still part of a region called the Midwest. They are not really in the middle of the west, but the nickname stuck.

Wisconsin is part of the Midwest region. Workers produce food such as corn and milk, make things people need, and ship food and other things on rivers and the Great Lakes. The land is mostly flat, with rolling hills.

Lesson 1 Memory Master
1. Name five landforms.
2. What kind of land does your region have? What cities? What rivers?

4. Western Upland

This land was never covered by Ice Age glaciers, so it still has high rocky ridges and many narrow valleys. People farm in the valleys. In the fall, the yellow oaks and red maple trees are beautiful. Most of the towns in this region are along the river.

5. Eastern Ridges and Lowlands

More people live in this region than in the others. Madison is our state capital. Milwaukee, Racine, and Green Bay are also large cities.

Because glaciers left fertile soil when they melted, there are many farms here. It is the richest *agricul-*

tural region in the state. Lake Winnebago and the shore of Lake Michigan make this region a great place to live or to visit.

How many different agricultural products can you see in this farm?

Madison is our state capital.

Have you visited Milwaukee?

▶ Farm and Madison photos by John D. Ivanko • Milwaukee photo by Ray F. Hillstrom Jr.

What Kind of Place is Wisconsin?

All places have a **natural environment**. The natural environment includes things such as land, rocks, trees, rivers, beaches, plants, and animals. Even air and the weather are part of the natural environment.

Places also have **human features**. Human features are things made by people. Cities and roads are human features. Farms and orchards are planted by people. They are human features, too. So are bridges and dams across rivers.

What do you think?

Name some natural and human features of the place where you live. Why are both important?

▲ Photo by Wisconsin Division of Tourism

What natural features do you see in this picture of a town in Northern Wisconsin? What human features do you see?

Taking Care of the Land

Our natural land is always changing. Some change is very slow. *Erosion* by wind and water slowly wears away rock and soil. Natural events, such as hurricanes and floods, happen fast. Sometimes, when there is a lot of rain, rivers and streams flood over the land.

People also change the land. They must have places to live and to work. They need lumber from trees and minerals from the ground. They need roads and bridges over rivers. Sometimes, though, if people are not careful, they can harm the air and the land. Their factories and cars can pollute the water and the air. Logging companies can cut down too many trees.

For many years, people earned money by cutting down trees and floating them down rivers to sawmills. Logs were sawed into lumber for buildings. The lumber produced in Wisconsin forests helped build cities like Milwaukee and Chicago.

The people who cut down the forests thought they would never run out of trees. People didn't know that cutting so many trees would change the land. After the trees were gone, however, rains washed away the rich soil. Fewer plants grew. Streams filled with soil and caused fish to die. The land that was once beautiful looked ugly.

Years later, logging companies started planting young trees when they cut down forests. People passed laws against polluting the air and water. They set aside land for state parks.

Laws sometimes stopped workers from building homes and freeways in places where wild animals lived. People set aside land for wildlife *refuges*. Laws protected some land so that it would stay natural forever. Today, more people try to keep our state and our country a beautiful place to live.

Children help plant trees in a park. How can you help our environment?

It will take many years before the trees grow back.

Copper Falls State Park is a place where people can enjoy nature.

◄ Tree photos by Sunny Walter

◄ Photo by Wisconsin Division of Tourism

Our Climate

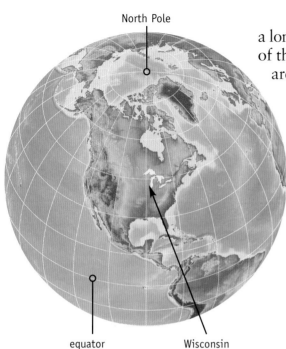

North Pole

equator   Wisconsin

Climate is very important. *Climate* is the weather of a place over a long time. The amount of rain or snow that falls in your yard is part of the climate. The temperatures in summer, winter, spring, and fall are part of climate.

Wisconsin temperatures can be as warm as 105 degrees and as cold as 30 degrees below zero. We often have heavy snows in winter. The snow is fun to play in, but your parents don't like to drive when it snows. It is dangerous!

During the spring and summer, we have thunderstorms. We see bright flashes of lightening and hear loud booms of thunder. Thunderstorms can be exciting, but they may bring hail or tornadoes.

What makes our climate what it is?

- **Distance from the equator** The equator is an imaginary line that goes around the center of the earth. Since it is the place closest to the sun, it is very hot near the equator. Wisconsin is not close to the equator. Our state is not close to either the North or South Pole, where there is ice all year long. This means that we have both hot and cold weather during the year.

- **Elevation** How high or low the land is above the level of the sea is called its *elevation*. When hikers climb higher and higher up a mountain, they feel the air getting cooler. In Wisconsin, there is only a difference of a little over 1,000 feet of elevation between our highest places and our lowest places. This is only as long as three football fields. Elevation does not affect Wisconsin's climate very much.

- **Nearness to large bodies of water** Water changes temperature slowly. This means that it stays warmer longer. Since the water in large lakes stays warmer longer, it keeps the land warmer, too. This is why cities such as Milwaukee and Green Bay, near Lake Michigan, are warmer in the winter than cities farther away from the lake. Since water also stays cool longer, cities near large lakes are cooler in the summer.

- **Location on the land** Winds change the temperature. Have you ever been enjoying a nice day, when all of a sudden the wind started to blow, and you got cold? Wisconsin is located in the center of North America. This means our weather is affected by cold winds sweeping in from Canada on the north and warm winds from the Gulf of Mexico to the south.

A puppy likes to play along the shore. The shores of Lake Michigan are the lowest elevation in Wisconsin. The large lake keeps the land near it warmer in the winter and cooler in the summer.

Winter snow means sledding! Every year, Wisconsin gets lots of snow.

Wisconsin's Plants

What kinds of plants grow naturally in Wisconsin? The next time you travel away from a city, look at the trees, bushes, grasses, weeds, and wildflowers that grow there. As you explore beaches, see what large and small plants live there. When you go to the mountains, see what different plants grow there. Notice how they change during different seasons of the year.

We have a slightly higher elevation and colder temperatures in the northern part of the state. This is why trees in northern Wisconsin are different from those in the south.

- In the north, most trees have needles. They are pine trees or fir trees. They are *conifers*. They stay green all year.
- In the south, most trees are *deciduous*. Their leaves fall off in the autumn. Maples, oaks, hickories, and poplars are very common deciduous trees. The southern part of the state also has prairie grasslands.

How many kinds of plants do you see in this place?

▶ Photo by John D. Ivanko

State Symbols

Tree: Sugar Maple

Flower:
Wood Violet

Deciduous trees lose their leaves every year.

Conifers have needles that stay green all year.

Everyone Loves Animals

Red fox

What animals do you have for pets? Do you have a bear or wolf? Do you have a pet deer or a pet raccoon? Of course not! They are wild animals. Smaller animals such as squirrels, chipmunks, foxes, opossums, and cottontail rabbits are also wild animals. They share a *habitat*. A habitat is the natural home of an animal.

Farmers raise animals for food. Animals like cows, hogs, and chickens are eaten for food. But most of Wisconsin's farm animals are cows that give milk for food. Wisconsin has the second largest number of milk cows in the United States. It produces about a third of all the cheese made in the whole country.

Black bear

Moose

Porcupine

White-tailed deer

▲ Red fox photo by John Lynn • Black bear photo by Middleton Evans • Moose and white-tailed deer photos by Jim Oltersdorf • Porcupine photo by Lynn Chamberlain

Going South for the Winter

Are you a bird watcher? Robins, red-winged blackbirds, and finches spend their summers in Wisconsin. You probably already know that when cold weather is coming, many birds go south where it is warmer. Marsh areas are important habitats for *migrating* birds. Ducks and geese feed at the marshes on their way south.

The Atlantic Flyway

Birds fly from Canada to warm places in South America every fall. Wisconsin is on one of the flyways.

Canada geese stop at Horican Marsh on their way north in the spring and south in the fall.

▶ Photo by Wisconsin Division of Tourism

▶ Baby duck photo by Jim Oltersdorf

Baby ducks live near lakes and streams.

State Symbols

Bird: Robin

Animal: Badger

Insect: Honey bee

Everything Moves

Wild animals move with the seasons. They go to find warmer or cooler places to live. They move to find food and water. When animals move, they often give plant seeds a ride to a new home. The seeds are stuck in animal fur and feathers.

People also travel from place to place. Sometimes they travel to see new places. They also move to find better places to live and work. They travel to visit relatives. When they travel, they share their ideas with other people.

Traveling gets faster all the time. In 1830, a trip from New York City to Wisconsin by stagecoach took four weeks. Today, that trip takes three hours by airplane.

People today travel farther than ever before. We meet people from many different states and countries. When you talk to someone on the telephone or send e-mail, you exchange ideas. Today, ideas can go across the planet in minutes.

Adults make and sell things to people in other places. Products such as lumber, cheese, cranberry juice, and beer are made in Wisconsin and sent all over the world. Our factories make tractors and other farm machines. Cars and motorcycles are shipped to other places. Do the adults in your family make or sell products? Do they send them to other places?

The next time you move, remember that movement is always going on. It is part of geography!

You Can Help!

It's up to everyone—even you—to help **conserve** natural resources and protect the environment. You can stop littering. You can pick up the things other people throw on the ground. You can recycle cans and paper. You can turn off lights and televisions when you aren't using them. You can wear a sweater instead of turning up the heat inside your home.

Everyone can be careful to take care of Wisconsin. Be an **advocate** of clean air and a clean land. Do your part to keep your state clean!

Ships dock at Lake Michigan and Lake Superior. They carry Wisconsin products to places all over the world.

Lesson 2 Memory Master

1. What does the natural environment include?
2. In what ways does the land change?
3. What things affect our climate?
4. The natural home of an animal is its _____.

What's the point?

Have you ever visited a forest, a farm, or a big city? Have you played outdoors when it was so cold you could hardly breathe? Have you seen a wild animal playing? Do you remember the bright colors of a sunset?

These things are all important to our state. A comfortable, beautiful place to live is important to us. Studying the land, animals, and plants helps us be more aware of taking care of these important things.

Chapter 2 Review

1. List five different landforms. (Remember, bodies of water are also landforms.)

2. What land region do you live in? What are its major cities?

3. List three features of the natural environment.

4. List three ways people have changed the environment.

5. List three things that affect our climate.

6. Name three kinds of plants that grow in our state.

7. Name three animals that live in our state.

8. Where do most birds fly to when winter is coming?

9. Name four things that move. How does movement change our land?

10. What can you do to help our land stay clean and beautiful?

Activity

Research and Write about Animals

There are so many great books about animals that you could never read them all. Choose an animal that lives in Wisconsin today or choose an Ice Age animal. Use an encyclopedia, library books, and a dictionary. Use the Internet, too. Find out all you can about the animal.

After you have done your research, write a story about the animal. Think of some words that describe your animal. Use some great action words that describe what your animal did. Draw a picture about your report. Tell the class what you learned.

Chapter 3

PEOPLE TO KNOW
Paleo People
Archaic People
Old Copper Culture
Mound Builders
   Hopewell People
   Mississippian People
Oneota

PLACES TO LOCATE
Mexico
Green Bay
La Crosse
Aztalan
Ohio River Valley
Atlantic Ocean
Gulf of Mexico
Lake Winnebago
Lake Koshkonog

American Indians have lived in North America
for thousands of years.
Photo by David Blanchette

timeline of events   13,000 B.C.   12,000 B.C.   11,000 B.C.   10,000 B.C.   9000 B.C.   8000 B.C.   7000

13,000–7000 B.C.
Paleo People

The First People

TERMS TO UNDERSTAND
ancestor
ancient
archaeologist
artifact
atlatl
charcoal
descendant
domesticate
effigy
nomadic
oral history
permanent
pitch
powwow
prehistoric
reverence
sapling
staple
wigwam

6000 B.C.	5000 B.C.	4000 B.C.	3000 B.C.	2000 B.C.	1000 B.C.	0	A.D. 1000	A.D. 2000

1500s
European explorers come to
Wisconsin.

1100–1400
Oneota

8000–500 B.C.
Archaic People

1000–500 B.C.
Old Copper Culture

100 B.C.–A.D. 1300
Mound Builders

100 B.C.–A.D. 300 Hopewell People
700–1200 Mississippian People
1100–1300 Aztalan is a permanent city.

The Earliest People

The people who lived here very long ago left no written records. We call these people *prehistoric*. How do we know about them?

The men, women, and children of long ago threw things away. They also dropped things. They left things behind when they moved. Today, when we find very old things people left behind, we call them *artifacts*. Artifacts are things such as spear points, tools, jewelry, baskets, and pottery.

Archaeologists

Archaeologists are scientists who study artifacts. The artifacts help us learn how the people lived.

Most *ancient* artifacts are buried in the earth. Over time, layers of sand and dirt have covered them up. Archaeologists must dig slowly and carefully to find the treasures. Sometimes only a small brush is gentle enough to clean off the dirt.

Once in a while, an amazing discovery is made. An archaeologist finds a sandal, rope, or piece of pottery that give new clues to how people lived long ago.

Archaeologists found a cave near La Crosse. It has many *charcoal* drawings. Archaeologists plan to spend the next several years studying the drawings. They will be searching for more clues to life in the past.

• La Crosse

Archaeologists dig very carefully. They try not to break tiny bones or artifacts that will help them learn about ancient people.

What do you think?

Do we always know how a person who lived thousands of years ago used an item? Can we guess how important a hair comb or a spear point was to a boy or girl? Why should scientists be careful about deciding how people in the past lived?

Paleo People

The earliest prehistoric people are called the Paleo People. Paleo means ancient. The people probably lived during the end of the Ice Age. They were *nomadic*. The men, women, and children walked from place to place to find food.

The people are called hunters and gatherers because they gathered seeds, berries, and roots from wild plants. The men hunted large animals such as mammoths with spears. They caught small animals such as rabbits and birds with nets or traps. They fished in streams and lakes.

Animals were important for clothing, too. The women used bone needles to sew animal hides together for clothes and blankets.

To make spears, clubs, and scrapers, the people sharpened rocks and tied them to wooden sticks. Sometimes they used a clamshell instead of a rock.

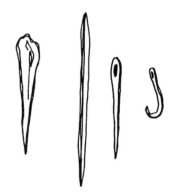

Sharp tools were made from animal bones.

Men used spears to kill mammoths and other large animals for food.

A sharp spear point made of flint was used to hunt large animals. Flint is a hard type of rock.

Archaic People

People who lived at a later time are called the Archaic People. Archaic means very old. The Archaic People were the ***descendants*** of the Paleo People. They were the great, great, great, great, great, great grandchildren of the Paleo People.

The climate had become dryer and warmer. The huge mammoths were gone from the land. The people hunted smaller animals such as deer, bears, ducks, and geese. Children helped find turtles, frogs, and shellfish. People caught fish in the lakes and rivers.

All parts of the animal were used. The flesh was used as food. Hides were made into clothing, moccasins, blankets, and bags. Bones and antlers were used for tools. Claws and teeth were sometimes made into necklaces.

Archaic People learned skills from their grandparents, parents, and from each other. They made better stone tools. They used the tools to chop down trees and make canoes. They made fishhooks and whistles from bones and antlers.

The Archaic People learned to use a spear thrower called an ***atlatl***.

Everything the people used was made from what they found in nature. This canoe was made by hollowing out a tree trunk. The inside of a large log was burned. Then the burned wood was scraped out. The men did this over and over until the canoe was ready.

Children helped gather nuts, berries, and plant roots for food.

Thin sheets of copper were pressed onto clay animals.

Old Copper Culture

The Old Copper Culture was a group of people who used copper to make weapons, tools, and jewelry. The people knew how to pound and hammer the copper into useful items. They did not mine the copper. They found it in lumps on the surface of the earth.

People traded tools and other objects they made with other groups of people. They traveled long distances in canoes to trade. Some copper artifacts have been found as far away as the Ohio River Valley.

The Mound Builders

The Mound Builders lived in thousands of villages along the rivers of what is today the Great Lakes region. Like the people before them, the Mound Builders hunted animals and gathered wild plants.

The Mound Builders didn't have to travel as much as earlier people. They learned how to grow crops and store food for the winter. They built **permanent** homes in large villages and cities. They stayed in the homes for years.

The people also made very large mounds of earth. Thousands of mounds have been found in Wisconsin. Some of the mounds were shaped to look like animals. These mounds are called **effigy** mounds. No one knows why the people shaped them like animals.

Some mounds may have been used for religious ceremonies. The village leader lived on top of the mound so he could be the closest to the sun and the sky. Some mounds were used like walls for protection from other groups of people and wild animals. Other mounds were made for burying the dead.

How did the people build the mounds? They dug the earth and carried it in baskets to the mound site. They probably walked up wooden ramps to pile the dirt higher and higher. The mounds were taller than many buildings today.

Mound Builder Sites

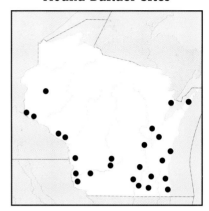

Thousands and thousands of mounds were built in Wisconsin. Each dot on the map shows sites where mounds were built. Do you live near any of the mound sites?

During the 1970s, college students built a mound. They used baskets to carry the dirt. Their teachers were amazed at how much dirt they could move in one day.

A burial mound looks like this today.

This drawing shows how a mound was made over the graves. As more people were buried, they were piled on top of each other and more dirt was added. The mounds grew higher and higher.

Linking the past to the present

Today, mounds are so covered with trees and bushes that you can drive right by and not even know you are near an ancient mound. You can't tell the difference between a large mound made by Mound Builders and a hill.

Aztalan
State Park •

Hopewell and Mississippian People

The Hopewell and the Mississippian people were Mound Builders who lived at different times. They came to Wisconsin to hunt and trade. They built small villages along rivers. There were hundreds of these villages along the Mississippi River. Mounds were part of the villages.

The Mississippian people built a large city. We call the city Aztalan. The city had mounds shaped like pyramids with flat tops. They looked like those built by the Aztec people in Mexico.

The people of Aztalan may have traded with the Aztecs. Trade routes covered thousands of miles. They went as far as the Atlantic Ocean and the Gulf of Mexico. The people traveled by canoes on the many rivers. They may also have walked a long way to trade with other groups of people. Sometimes traders were gone from home for months and even years.

Aztalan lasted almost two hundred years. The people of Aztalan were probably the *ancestors* of some modern American Indians, including the Winnebago.

Children at Aztalan lived in homes like these. Can you tell what they were made of?

The Temple Mound at Aztalan still stands today.

The Oneota

The Oneota might be descendants of the people at Aztalan. Most of our understanding of the Oneota comes from artifacts found at campsites and burial sites. Oneota pottery looks like the pottery of the Aztalan people.

The Oneota set up villages around Green Bay, Lake Winnebago, Lake Koshkonong, and La Crosse. They planted gardens. They grew vegetables like pumpkins, squash, corn, and beans. They dried the foods so that they could be eaten in the winter. This meant that families did not have to move around so much to find food.

Lesson 1 Memory Master
1. Scientists who dig for ancient artifacts are called _____.
2. Who were the earliest people who lived at the end of the Ice Age?
3. What tools helped the Archaic People get food?
4. List three ways mounds were used.

Recording History

By the time the European explorers came to Wisconsin, many Indian groups were living here. The groups included the Menominee, Dakota, Winnebago, Kickapoo, Sauk, Fox, and others.

The explorers wrote in their journals what the Indian people looked like. They wrote what the people ate and what their homes were like. They learned the names of some of the Indian people and wrote about them. Some explorers even drew pictures of Indian people and their villages.

Because we have some written histories about them, we call later groups historic Indians. Their artifacts are still important, but the journals give even more clues to how the people lived. You will read more about the explorers who wrote about the Indians in the next chapter.

Oral History

Early people remembered their history by telling stories to their children, grandchildren, and to each other. Their history was passed down by word of mouth. It was not written on paper. This spoken history is called *oral history*.

Linking the past to the present
Today, we have many history books. People, however, still tell their history, or what happened to them, to others. What ways have you shared your history with someone else?

Lesson 2

Historic Indians

WORDS TO UNDERSTAND
domesticate
oral history
pitch
powwow
reverence
sapling
staple
wigwam

New Groups Come

More and more settlers were moving into the towns on the East Coast of America. They lived on land that American Indians had used for hunting grounds. As the population grew larger in the East, many Indian groups went west.

The Potawatomi and the Chippewa Indians came to the Great Lakes from Canada. Soon there were so many new people living here, they pushed other groups out. The Mesquakie moved into Iowa. The Kickapoo moved to Illinois.

As large groups of people moved, there were often wars between the people who already lived here and the new group. The longest wars were between the Dakotas and the Chippawas. Those wars lasted over a hundred years. In the end, the Chippawas lived all over the land north and east of the Mississippi River.

Wars were terrible. Many men were killed in battles. Sometimes whole villages, including old people and children, were forced to walk away from their homes. Often they did not have food to take with them. They had no protection from the cold. Many died on the trip.

What do you think?

Everyone needs a place to live and work. Was it right for settlers from Europe to move onto Indian lands in the East? Was it right for the Indian groups there to move onto land used by other Indian groups in Wisconsin? Can you think of peaceful ways the people could have solved the problems?

What's in a Name?

The Chippewa gained their name from the way they stitched their moccasins. A seam around the toe looked puckered. "Chippewa" meant puckered.

In Minnesota and Canada, the Chippewa call themselves Ojibwa. In Wisconsin, Chippewa is the more common name.

All Chippewa also call themselves the Anishanabeg—the first people.

The Chippewa called their enemies Dakota, which meant "snake in the grass."

Families and Bands

The family was very important to the Native Americans. Parents and children lived together. Sometimes one set of grandparents also lived with the family. For hunting and food-gathering trips, several villages lived together in a band.

Solving Problems

Each band was responsible for its own people. The band was run by a council of elders. The elders were men who were wise and thoughtful. They had proved that they could make good decisions.

The council did not rule. It guided the people. When there was a problem in the band, the people talked about it. Very important ideas often involved a whole village. Both men and women spoke and tried to solve problems.

People respected their leaders.

Finding Food

Native American groups moved with the changing seasons to find food. Each band had its own gathering places. In the summer, there were plenty of berries and seeds to gather and wild animals to hunt. Native Americans hunted deer, beaver, ducks, geese, and other animals. They fished in the many rivers and lakes. They gathered wild foods and planted crops.

Winter could be very hard if the food ran out and the hunting was bad. February was the hardest month. The February moon was called the "hungry moon."

Wild Rice and Maple Sugar

Wild rice was a *staple* in the peoples' diet. They ate it almost every day. Wild rice is a type of grass that grows in shallow areas of lakes. Wild rice was cooked and dried. The rice could also be ground into flour. Rice could be mixed with maple sugar.

In the spring, the people harvested maple sap. They boiled the sap until it thickened. At that point, it turned into maple syrup. The thick syrup was put in birch bark containers to dry into maple sugar.

A band returned each year to the same maple tree grove to gather sap and to the same lake to gather wild rice. Other groups entered these places only with permission.

▶ Photo by Wisconsin Division of Tourism

Wild rice grows in shallow parts of lakes. It is still harvested today.

Naming the Seasons

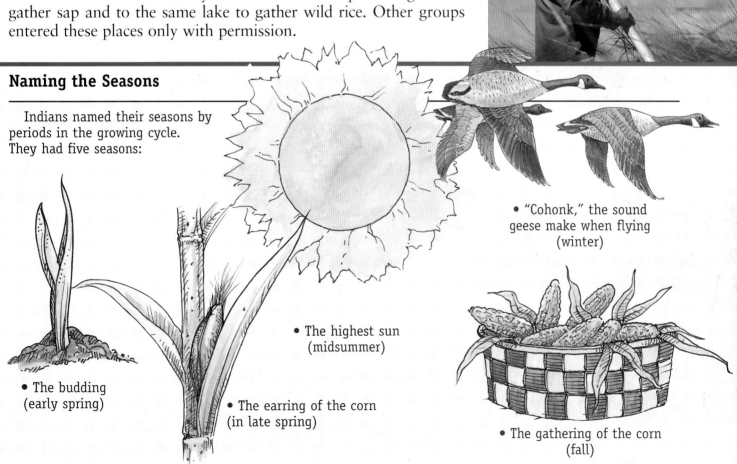

Indians named their seasons by periods in the growing cycle. They had five seasons:

- The budding (early spring)
- The earring of the corn (in late spring)
- The highest sun (midsummer)
- "Cohonk," the sound geese make when flying (winter)
- The gathering of the corn (fall)

Called the "three sisters," corn, beans, and squash were planted together.

Domesticating Plants and Animals

When people learn how to grow a wild plant, we say that plant has been *domesticated.* Corn has been domesticated for thousands of years. In fact, corn cannot grow without the help of people.

Native Americans ate green corn. Green corn is another name for corn on the cob. The season was too short for the corn to fully ripen. Have you eaten green corn?

Animals can be domesticated, too. Native Americans in Wisconsin domesticated only one animal—the dog. They used dogs to pull loads, and sometimes for food. Dogs were pets, too.

What do you think?

Why do you think the domestication of plants and animals was important? Do you think life became easier or harder when plants and animals were domesticated?

Once cameras were invented, photographers took pictures of American Indians in fancy clothes. Everyday clothes were usually much more simple.

Clothing

No plant in Wisconsin had fibers that could be made into cloth. All clothes were made from animal skins. The men hunted the animals. The women scraped the fur off the skins. Next, they softened the skins and cut them into pieces. Finally, the women sewed or laced skins together with bone needles.

In the winter, people wore long leather shirts, leggings, and moccasins. Sometimes clothing for special times was decorated with colored porcupine quills or painted with dyes.

In the summer, people wore fewer clothes. Young children often did not wear anything at all.

Homes

The people lived in several kinds of houses. During the fall, winter, and spring, they lived in *wigwams.* The bowl-shaped house had a frame of small branches. Mats of woven grasses or birch bark were then tied to the framework.

When the people moved to a new place, they took off the mats. They rolled them up and carried them to the new place. Since families returned to the same areas each year, the old frames were fixed and used again.

During the summer when the band gathered to grow crops and gather food, larger wooden houses were built.

A Step-by-Step Wigwam

1 To build a wigwam, the people cut down straight young trees called *saplings*. They trimmed off the branches. Then they dug holes in the ground. They put saplings in the holes. This held the saplings in place.

2 They bent the saplings over, then lashed them together with cord, vines, or animal skins. This made a frame for the wigwam.

3 Finally, the people covered the frame with bark or mats made of grasses and reeds. They left a door and a hole in the top so the smoke from the fire could escape.

Birch Bark

People made many useful objects from birch bark. The bark was collected by peeling it in sheets from the tree trunk. The large sheets were often several feet in both length and width.

Birch bark canoes were perfect for travel on lakes and rivers. They moved easily and silently through the water. The canoes didn't weigh very much. Men could carry them over land when they needed to go from one river to another. The canoes worked so well that they were copied by other tribes and later by European explorers.

To make canoes, birch bark was tied to a wooden frame. The seams were sealed with sticky **pitch** from pine trees.

Other items were also made from birch bark. Women made bark boxes to hold corn, wild rice, and other items. The boxes were coated with pitch to make them waterproof. Some boxes were decorated by cutting patterns into the bark.

People cooked in the boxes by filling them with very hot rocks and water. When the water got very hot, meat and vegetables were added. The food cooked in the hot water.

People used birch bark canoes to travel on the many rivers in Wisconsin.

"We shake down acorns and pine nuts. We don't chop down the trees. We use only dead wood for fires. . . . But the white people plow up the ground, pull down the trees, and the tree says, 'Don't. I am sore. Don't hurt me.'"

—Indian woman

A Spiritual People

Like all people, Native Americans had a set of beliefs about how life began and what happens to us after we die. They were very careful about how they treated the natural world around them. Each animal and plant had a spirit and should be treated with *reverence*. The earth, the rocks, the sun, the moon, and the stars also had spirits. There were beliefs about how people should treat each other.

The people believed in a spirit world. This world was a beautiful and wonderful place. People tried to connect with this spirit world through hours of prayer and dance. It was believed that people who saw the spirit world were given special powers to heal the sick and see the future.

The sweat lodge was an important part of spiritual life. The lodge was a small wigwam with a fire and hot rocks inside. Water was sprinkled on the rocks to make steam. A man stayed in the sweat lodge until he was sweating all over. Then he ran out of the lodge and into the snow or a river. Sometimes a group would sit in the lodge together and get instruction from religious leaders. People said they felt clean and relaxed after being in the lodge. Their minds were opened to spiritual guidance.

Animals and Birds

American Indians shared the land with animals and birds.
They did not step on a snake's tracks in the sand.
They did not disturb a fox's den.
They did not push a lizard out of the path.

Trees, flowers, rabbits, and insects were all important.
American Indians said the land belonged to
the spider and the ant and the deer,
the same as it does to people.

Myths and Legends

Most American Indians had legends and stories that told their history. Sometimes the stories told how the tribe came to be. They answered questions in nature, such as why owls stay up at night or why the fox is so sly. They told of animals and spirits coming to teach or help the people. The legends taught children lessons and values such as honesty and respect.

The people did not write down legends. They told and re-told them out loud. A good story-teller was an honored member of the tribe.

How the Sky and Earth Were Created

When Grandfather Sun was young, he was alone. He felt lonely because the stars were far away. He danced all by himself in his great fire and sang his songs all alone.

Then the Sun heard a pretty song coming from somewhere below him. He looked down and saw two lovely sisters dancing and singing sweetly. They were Grandmother Moon and Grandmother Ocean. They were young then. The Moon was dark and full of mystery. Her dance rose and fell in a rhythm. The Ocean was bright and calm. Her dance moved slowly around her sister.

When the Sun saw the sisters and heard them singing, he was happy. He did not want them to leave. And so the Sun married the Ocean. Her sister the Moon also danced and sang around the Sun's warm fire.

The Sun's energy reflected off the waters of the Ocean in a song. From this song, Father Sky was born. He embraced his mother, the Ocean. He reached up to his father, the Sun. Soon Mother Earth rose up from the Ocean and joined her brother in a song of the world.

—Adapted from "The Song of Creation" in *Children of the Morning Light*, as told by Manitonquat

Games and Dancing

Adults and children enjoyed playing games. They often played a game that the French later called lacrosse. Each player held a stick with a scoop on the end. A ball was passed through the air from player to player.

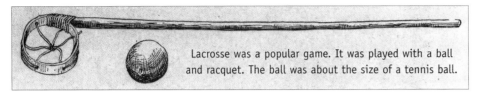

Lacrosse was a popular game. It was played with a ball and racquet. The ball was about the size of a tennis ball.

People enjoyed being together. They loved to dance to the beat of a drum. Dances were held for special ceremonies, as a sign of the changing seasons, or for fun.

Powwow

A *powwow* was a gathering, a celebration, a fair, and a contest all rolled up into one big event. People celebrated marriages and births at pow-wows.

Children and young people met friends, played games, and danced. There were many kinds of wonderful food to eat. People could buy clothes, jewelry, and many other items at a powwow.

Powwows lasted from one day to a week. Today, some people travel all summer from one powwow to another across the Midwest and the Great Plains.

Today, Native Americans get together at a powwow. Children dress in native costumes, dance, play music, and eat traditional food.

Photo by Wisconsin Division of Tourism

Lesson 2 Memory Master
1. List four historic groups of Wisconsin Indians.
2. What foods did the people eat?
3. What type of house did the people live in most of the year?
4. What things did the people make from birch bark?
5. What is a legend?

Activity

Moccasin Game

Many people in North America played the moccasin game. The game depended on memory and teamwork.

Two teams play the game. Teams can be made up of one or more persons. Each team has a loader and a shooter.

Supplies:

- four moccasins or pieces of animal skin (pieces of heavy cloth)

- four small objects (shells, beads, or marbles)

- 20 short sticks (Popsicle sticks)

- one long stick (yardstick)

- a blanket or rug

These ceremonial moccasins were worn by Lone Bear. They were decorated with colorful beads. You will learn how the Native Americans got beads in the next chapter.

Rules:

1) The teams sit at opposite ends of the rug.

2) The shooters turn their backs to the game.

3) The loader hides the object under one of the four moccasins.

4) The shooter turns around and uses the stick to do one of two things:
   a. "shoot straight"—points to the moccasin that is believed to hide the object or
   or
   b. lifts a moccasin believed *not* to hide the object and places it on top of another moccasin. The shooter may do this until one moccasin remains.

5) The shooter has ten counters.
   a. If the shooter guesses incorrectly, he or she gives up the number of counters matching the number of moccasins left on the blanket. (If he shoots straight and is wrong, he loses four counters.)
   b. If the shooter selects correctly, he or she gets the number of counters matching the moccasins left. (If the shooter selects correctly the first time, he or she gets four counters.)

6) The teams trade roles as shooters and loaders.

7) The first side to gain all twenty counters wins.

8) If teams are used, the shooters can give each other hints using signals but are not allowed to talk.

From *The Moccasin Game*, American Indian Language and Culture Education Board, Madison, Wisconsin

What's the point?

By studying people who lived before us, we discover that all people have the same needs. We all need food, clothing, and shelter. Families and friends are important to all of us.

The early people of Wisconsin developed many useful skills that later people used. They learned how to build homes, how to domesticate certain plants and animals, and how to make tools and weapons. Each group improved these basic skills.

Early Native Americans drew pictures on rock walls.

Chapter 3 Review

1. The first group of people who lived here are called the _____ People.

2. The second group of people who lived here are called the _____ People.

3. Name three foods that Paleo and Archaic People ate.

4. What is the Old Copper Culture known for?

5. The Mound Builders buried their dead in mounds made of _____ .

6. List three things you learned about the Mound Builders.

7. What is the difference between written and oral histories?

8. What was the hardest time of the year for people to find food?

9. What crop has been domesticated for thousands of years?

10. List at least two things Indian people enjoyed doing together.

Geography Tie-In

Find out if there were any groups of Mound Builders who lived near you. See if you can find information about Mound Builder sites on the Internet. (Hint: Sometimes it is spelled moundbuilders.) Visit an actual site or museum if you can.

THE TIME
1600s–1700s

PEOPLE TO KNOW
Claude Jean Allouez
Etienne Brule
Jean Nicolet
Jacques Marquette
Louis Joliet
Rene Menard

PLACES TO LOCATE
Europe
Great Britain
France
Canada
Quebec
Montreal
Green Bay
Prairie du Chien
Ashland
Portage
Allegheny Mountains
Atlantic Ocean
Great Lakes
Lake Winnebago
St. Lawrence River
Mississippi River
Wisconsin River
Fox River
Arkansas River
Gulf of Mexico

Missionaries, Traders, and Indians

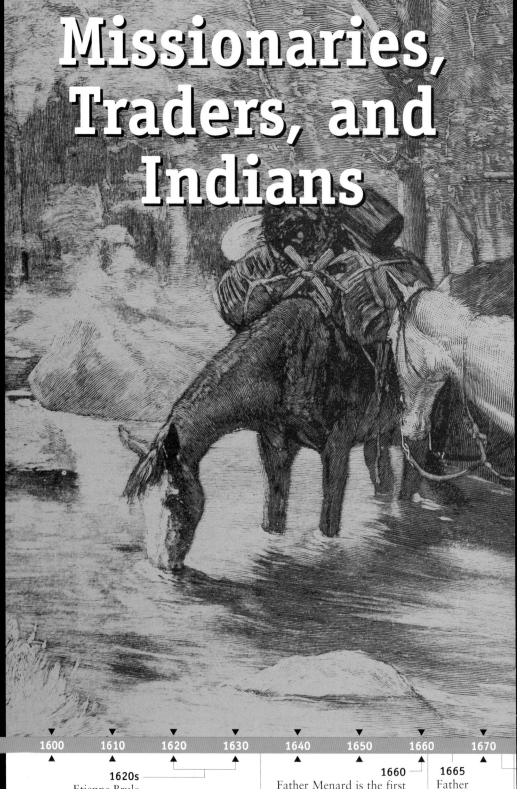

timeline of events

1600	1610	1620	1630	1640	1650	1660	1670

1620s
Etienne Brule
explores Lake
Superior region.

1634
Jean Nicolet
arrives in
Wisconsin.

1660
Father Menard is the first
Jesuit priest in Wisconsin.

1661
Father Menard dies
in the woods.

1665
Father
Allouez
arrives
to work
with
Indians.

WORDS TO UNDERSTAND
ally
barter
cargo
Christian
claim
colony
convert
empire
Jesuit
merchant
mission
pelt
portage
poverty
rival
translator
voyageur
wilderness

Fur trappers were also called mountain men. They were some of the earliest explorers.
The men set traps for beavers and other wild animals and sold the furs.
Art by Frederic Remington

Copyright 1890 by
FREDERIC REMINGTON

1680	1690	1700	1710	1720	1730	1740	1750	1760	1770	1780	1790

1763
Proclamation of 1763
is made by the British.

1673
Father Jacques Marquette and Louis Joliet
begin their expedition.

First French fort is built at Prairie du Chien.

1675
Father Marquette dies.

1754–1763
French and Indian War

1760
British take over Canada and
the Great Lakes Region.

1764
First English settlement
is built at Green Bay.

Lesson **1**

Early Explorers

PEOPLE TO KNOW
Claude Jean Allouez
Etienne Brule
Louis Joliet
Jacques Marquette
Rene Menard
Jean Nicolet

PLACES TO LOCATE
Europe
France
Great Britain
Canada
Quebec
Montreal
Green Bay
Prairie du Chien
Ashland
Portage
The Great Lakes
Lake Winnebago
Mississippi River
Arkansas River
Wisconsin River
Fox River
Gulf of Mexico

WORDS TO UNDERSTAND
cargo
Christian
claim
colony
convert
empire
Jesuit
mission
portage
poverty
translator
wilderness

A New World

After a long journey across the Atlantic Ocean, Columbus and his crew landed on an island near Florida. When Columbus returned to Spain, he told people there about the wonderful new land of America. Over two hundred years later, much of our continent was *claimed* by three countries—Spain, Great Britain (England), and France. These countries were all in Europe, far across the Atlantic Ocean.

European governments claimed the land, but hardly any British, French, or Spanish people lived here. Who did live here? Millions of American Indian people lived all over America.

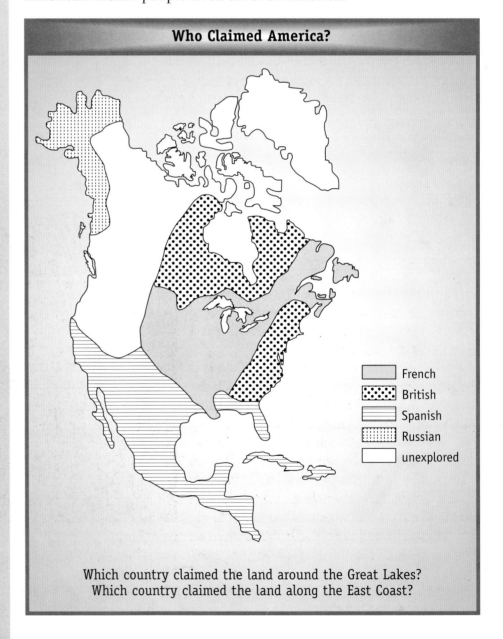

Who Claimed America?

French
British
Spanish
Russian
unexplored

Which country claimed the land around the Great Lakes?
Which country claimed the land along the East Coast?

The French Explorers

The French dreamed of a huge *empire* in North America. They wanted to control as much of the land as they could. Great Britain already had *colonies* along the Atlantic Coast. A colony is a community that is ruled by a larger country far away.

French explorers wanted to learn more about the New World. They crossed the Atlantic Ocean on wooden ships with tall white sails. They started colonies in Quebec and Montreal in what is now called Canada.

Brule

A young Frenchman named Etienne Brule lived with the Huron Indians and explored the land around Lake Superior. He may have been the first white man to see Wisconsin. He did not leave journals about his trips or the American Indians he met.

Other explorers wrote that "Brule dressed like an Indian . . . and learned their language very well." Years later, Brule was killed by the Huron.

Nicolet

About fifteen years later, Jean Nicolet wanted to find a water route that went all the way to China. If such a river could be found, ships could travel to China and sell things made in Europe. On the trip back, sailors could bring beautiful soft silk and spices from China. It would have been a good way to make money.

Nicolet and his friends paddled canoes across Lake Michigan. They stopped on the shore of Green Bay. Hoping that the local Winnabago Indians might show him a way to China, he wore a colorful Chinese robe. The Indians had never seen such clothes before! They had never felt silk. Nicolet didn't know that a whole continent and a whole ocean were between him and China.

Nicolet wore a Chinese robe to greet the Indians. He fired loud shots into the air from two guns.

Nicolet lived with the Indians and learned their language. They helped him explore Lake Michigan and Green Bay. Finally, tired from months of travel, Nicolet went back to Quebec. Years later, the French built their first trading post at Green Bay, close to where Nicolet had first landed.

Joliet and Marquette

The French were interested in any water route that would make travel easier. The French governor sent Louis Joliet (joh le ET) to find out where the Mississippi River led. Joliet was an expert mapmaker.

Jacques Marquette (mar KET), a Catholic priest, was asked to go along. Father Marquette had lived in Canada for seven years and had learned to speak many Indian languages.

Joliet and Marquette and five men traveled in birch bark canoes across Lake Michigan. They stopped at Green Bay, then paddled up the Fox River to Lake Winnebago. When the canoes could go no farther, the Indians helped the French carry, or *portage*, their boats. They carried the boats and their *cargo* on their backs until they reached the Wisconsin River. Then the two Indian guides left. They were afraid of what might be ahead.

The men traveled on the Wisconsin River until it flowed into the Mississippi River. At the place where the two rivers joined, the French built a settlement. They named it Prairie du Chien. The name meant "prairie of dogs."

Down the Mississippi River

The men followed the Mississippi south. After many days, they stopped for a peaceful meeting with some Indians who gave them a peace pipe that later saved their lives. At the Arkansas River, Indian men with guns suddenly surrounded them. Only the sight of the Indian peace pipe kept the Indians from attacking.

The Indians told Marquette that the guns had come from other white men about ten day's journey away. The other men were probably Spanish, and it would be dangerous to go on. The Indians also told the men that the Mississippi flowed to the Gulf of Mexico.

Marquette and Joliet claimed all of the land on both sides of the Mississippi River for France. Then they went back to Canada with exciting news. They had discovered that it was possible to travel from Canada all the way to the Gulf of Mexico by water. This was a very important discovery because traveling by water was so much easier than traveling by land.

The brave explorers had also discovered a land with rolling hills and wide valleys. There were thick forests, beautiful lakes, and many rivers. Thousands of beavers lived in the rivers. Other animals with thick furs lived in the forests. It was a good place to trap for furs.

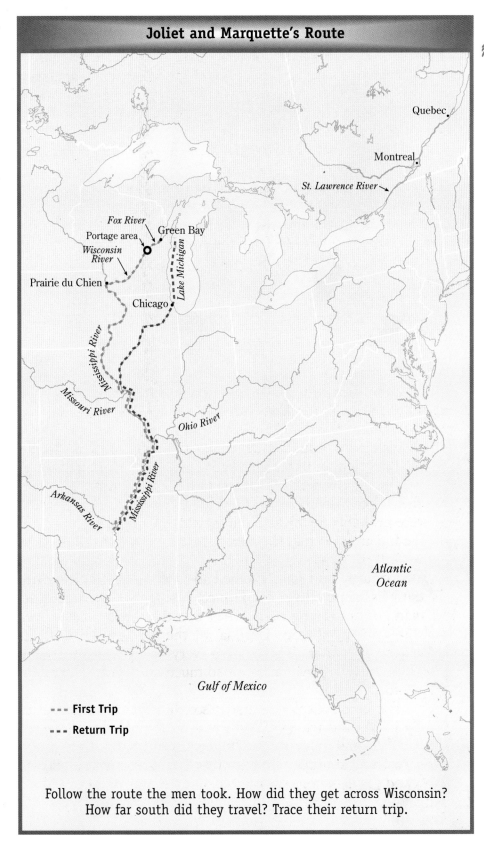

Joliet and Marquette's Route

Quebec

Montreal

St. Lawrence River

Fox River
Portage area — Green Bay
Wisconsin
River
Prairie du Chien
Chicago
Lake Michigan

Mississippi River

Missouri River

Ohio River

Arkansas River

Mississippi River

Atlantic
Ocean

Gulf of Mexico

- - - **First Trip**
- - - **Return Trip**

Follow the route the men took. How did they get across Wisconsin?
How far south did they travel? Trace their return trip.

WISCONSIN
P·O·R·T·R·A·I·T

Jacques Marquette
1637-1675

Jacques Marquette was born in France. He was a gentle, kind boy. When he was seventeen years old, he became a priest. He wanted to be a missionary overseas. His wish came true when he was sent to Canada. There he taught the Indians, studied their languages, and started several missions.

While teaching the Indians, Marquette learned of a great river to the west. He also met Louis Joliet. When he was thirty-six years old, Marquette went with Joliet and other men to explore the great river the Indians had spoken of. They were the first Europeans to see the upper Mississippi River. (The Spanish had claimed the lower part.)

Marquette wrote a journal about his trip on the river.

"We safely entered Mississippi on the 17th of June, with a joy I cannot express."

A few years later, while Marquette was traveling to see his friends, the Illinois Indians, he became ill and died. He was only thirty-eight years old.

**Marquette University
in Milwaukee is named
for Father Marquette.**

Milwaukee •

Ashland

Green Bay •

Catholic Missionaries

Jesuits were Catholic priests. They left France and other countries and came to the American *wilderness* to teach Indians. The priests were usually young men who took vows to live in *poverty* and serve God by helping other people. Priests built *missions*, which were like churches where the people could be taught. The priests lived at the missions, too.

The priests, who were called Black Robes by Native Americans, tried to teach the Indian people about Jesus Christ and baptize them as *Christians*. The priests did *convert* some Indians. They also helped them when they were sick. They learned Indian languages and used this skill to keep peace between the tribes. They also served as *translators* between Indians and white people.

Father Menard

The first Jesuit missionary to teach the Wisconsin Indians was Father Rene Menard. He started a mission at Chequamegon Bay near what is now Ashland.

He died while taking some food to the starving Huron Indians. His friend said he had stepped ashore to lighten the canoe and was never seen again by white men. His prayer book and robe were later found with the Dakota Indians.

Father Allouez

The second missionary was very important to the Native Americans. Father Claude Jean Allouez arrived at Chequamegon Bay and taught many different tribes. He learned to speak at least ten Indian languages.

While he lived with the Indians, he wrote many things about them and sent his reports back to France.

These reports helped other people learn about how the Indians lived.

Life was very hard for Father Allouez. He walked many miles, meeting with Indian people wherever he went. He slept on the ground with a fur robe for a blanket. Food was hard to find.

We were forced to eat moss growing upon the rocks. It is a sort of shell-shaped leaf that is always covered with caterpillars and spiders; and which, on being boiled, makes a black soup.

Father Allouez helped Indians build a mission on Madeline Island. Later they built a mission near the Fox River. That mission later became the first real town for white settlers in Wisconsin. It is now known as the city of Green Bay.

▶ Photo by Lynn Chamberlain

Lesson 1 Memory Master

1. Who was the first white man to enter the Wisconsin region?
2. Who was the explorer who tried to find a water route to China?
3. Which two men were sent to explore the Mississippi River?
4. Why did the Jesuit priests come to Wisconsin?

The Fur Trade

Soon other French men came to America. Most of them were trappers and traders. They wanted beaver fur to sell in Europe.

Fur trading companies were formed in Montreal and Quebec. Many people worked in the fur trade. Each fall, traders in canoes set out for the Great Lakes. Their canoes were filled with goods to trade to the Indians for furs.

During the fall and winter, Native Americans set traps in the snow and in the icy rivers. The Indians killed the animals and cut off the soft thick *pelts*. They stretched the pelts so they would keep their shape. In the spring, Indian men sold the pelts to the French.

Beaver pelts were so valuable that the fur was sometimes called "soft gold."

French trappers also trapped beavers, mink, fox, squirrel, and raccoon. The French took tall piles of furs back to Canada. They loaded the pelts on ships that took them to France. Many people in Europe wanted the thick furs.

Good relations with the Indians helped the fur trade. Both groups were happy to get things they wanted in exchange for furs. Few Frenchmen became farmers. Instead, many hoped to get rich in the fur trade.

Lesson 2

Trappers and Traders

PLACES TO LOCATE
Great Britain
France
Montreal
Quebec
The Great Lakes

WORDS TO UNDERSTAND
ally
barter
merchant
pelt
rival
voyageur

Bartering

Trading what you have for what you want is called *bartering*. People bartered for things they needed instead of using money to buy them.

Merchants are people who buy and sell things. Merchants came to the Great Lakes region. Usually merchants were also explorers and trappers. They built log trading posts. Indians traded animal furs for metal pots, knives, guns, and needles. Colorful glass beads, cloth, and blankets were also popular trade items. Even food was bartered.

Indian women grew corn and traded it for French goods. Indian boys caught and dried fish for the French.

High Fashion

For over 100 years, tall felt hats were the fashion for European gentlemen. Hat makers could hardly keep up with all the hats people wanted. The felt was made from beaver fur.

People wanted fur for other reasons, too. It was popular for both men and women to wear fox, otter, and other animal fur on coat collars, sleeves, gloves, and boots.

The trappers in Europe had killed all the beavers there. When they learned that the land in America had rivers full of beavers, they came here to trap them. Beaver hats were the reason our land was explored by trappers.

This house in Prairie du Chien was built with money from the fur trade.

Linking the past to the present

During the 150 years that French traders were in our region, they named places that still have French names today. Some of them are La Crosse, Eau Claire, Fond du Lac, and Flambeau. Can you think of other places in our state with French names?

The Amazing Voyageurs

Bundles of furs were stored until trading companies came to Canada to collect them. The men who carried the furs to trading posts along the rivers were called *voyageurs*. The men paddled the canoes and did other hard jobs.

The canoes were big enough to hold eight men and their cargo. Birch bark canoes were used because they were easy to build and repair. They could float in very shallow water, even when filled with heavy cargo. The canoes were light enough to be carried.

Native Americans often worked as guides for the voyageurs. They helped them find their way.

Photo of house in Prairie du Chien by Wisconsin Division of Tourism

Often eight men spent fifteen hours a day paddling a long canoe. The canoes were so full of furs that the men could hardly move. To help pass the time, the men sang. They paddled the canoes to the rhythm of the songs.

The voyageurs showed pride in their work by the way they dressed and decorated their canoes. They dressed in deerskin shirts, leggings, and moccasins. Canoes were brightly painted. Sometimes feathers hung on the front and the back.

Often the rivers and lakes did not connect to each other. The voyageurs had to portage their cargo over the land to the next body of water. They carried ninety-pound bundles of furs, sometimes as far as five miles. Some men carried more than one bundle at a time. The hard work of the voyageurs helped make the fur trade successful.

Today, the town of Portage is located on the Wisconsin River. It is the place where traders carried furs over land.

Portage ●

The French and Indian War

The French and the Native Americans had customs and habits that were very different from each other's. Most disagreements were settled peacefully, however. Both sides wanted to keep trading with each other.

Two countries in Europe—France and Great Britain—did not solve their problems peacefully. France and Great Britain had been *rivals* for many years. Each was trying to win the race to claim the most land around the Great Lakes. Both countries believed claiming the land would make them rich and powerful. It was the final contest to decide who had the most power in the New World.

Indians helped the French fight the British. They often killed English settlers.

Great Britain is a group of countries called the British Isles. England was one of those countries. This is why English people are often called British.

A New Rule

Great Britain made a new rule. It was called the Proclamation of 1763. It gave western lands to the Indians. Only special traders could go into the Indian lands.

This rule angered many of the English colonists on the coast because they wanted the western land. Many colonists believed that the Indians did not deserve so much land. They ignored the rules and crossed into Indian lands anyway.

French explorers were the first white people to explore the Great Lakes and much of the Mississippi River. They claimed a huge part of North America, including what is now Wisconsin. Their traders and missionaries had worked hard to explore and control the land. France felt it belonged to them.

Different groups of American Indians were *allies*, or friends, of both countries. Many Indians sided with the French. Others fought with the British. For nine years, the two countries fought over who owned the land. Neither side thought the Native Americans owned the land.

Peace at Last

The war finally ended when the British captured Quebec and Montreal. A peace treaty was signed. It gave the British control of Canada and all French lands east of the Mississippi River. The land that would someday become Wisconsin was now in British hands.

Linking the past to the present

When Great Britain won the war, the British ruled the area of Wisconsin. If France had won the war, do you think we might speak French instead of English today?

Life After the War

The English continued the fur trade in Wisconsin. They used many of the trapping and trading methods the French had used. Many of the French traders stayed and worked for the British. Prairie du Chien became an important trading post where traders sold their pelts and bought supplies for their next trip.

The traders did more than trade. They visited with other traders and enjoyed all kinds of sports. Trading posts also had churches where voyageurs often married Native American women. Children were baptized there. During the winter, school was held. Usually a priest was the teacher, but sometimes a trading post clerk taught classes.

Fur trading was a successful business. Most of the voyageurs lived comfortable lives in the villages and never returned to France. The years of the French trade empire ended, but the adventures of the explorers and traders would not be forgotten.

What do you think?

When the French came into the Wisconsin region, they changed the Indians' lifestyle. How did they do this? In what ways do you think the Indians also changed the lifestyle of the Europeans?

A New Lifestyle for the American Indians

Imagine meeting people you did not even know existed. That is what happened when the boys and girls in an Indian village met French missionaries or traders. It must have seemed strange and exciting.

The men from Europe had lighter skin, they had beards, and they spoke a different language. They showed the children things made from metal that the children had never seen before. Metal guns could kill a deer with a loud bang. Metal knives cut quickly. The children liked the colored beads the traders gave them. They had never seen glass before.

After the Indians met the traders, mothers decorated special clothes with glass beads in different sizes, colors, and patterns.

Clothing styles changed, too. An Indian girl had only worn clothing made from soft animal skins. The traders brought woven cloth. It was light to hold. It even came in colors! Wool blankets were traded, too, and used instead of fur robes.

Not all the changes were good. After the missionaries and traders came, something terrible happened in Indian villages. First the old people, then the youngest children, then adults died from new diseases. Measles, flu, and smallpox had come to the New World. A man from Europe might get very sick and die from measles or flu, but he often got better. His body was more used to the germs. But when Indian children got smallpox, they usually died.

Lesson 2 Memory Master

1. What were trappers looking for in Wisconsin?
2. What work did the voyageurs do?
3. What were France and Great Britain fighting for in the French and Indian War?

What's the point?

The French explorers told people about the beautiful land they had discovered. Missionaries came to teach and help American Indians. Fur traders came to get beaver pelts. They bartered with the Indians for furs. The French named places that still have French names. Maybe one of them is your city.

The French explorers discovered rivers and lakes that are still used to ship products that you buy at the store. The British also wanted the rich lands and the fur trade, and fought a war to get them. The French and the English changed the lifestyle of the American Indians. Life in Wisconsin was changed forever.

Activity

A Chain of Events

In history, one thing leads to another. In this lesson:

- Men in Europe wore tall felt hats made of beaver fur.

- Traders came to Wisconsin to get beaver fur.

- Indian men trapped the beaver.

- Indians traded pelts for metal tools and glass beads.

- Voyageurs took bundles of furs to Canada.

- Ships took furs from Canada to Europe and sold them.

- The fur was made into tall felt hats.

On a piece of paper, draw a large circle. Then draw seven smaller circles around the edge. In each smaller circle, draw a simple picture of each of the events on the list. Then write in a few words to explain each drawing. Put an arrow from one circle to the next. This is your chain of events. It happened over and over again.

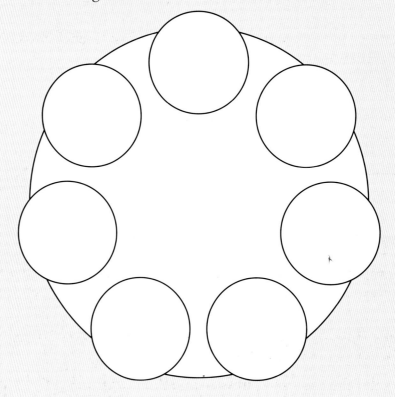

Activity

Weighing In

1. Weigh this book. Then figure out how many books it would take to equal ninety pounds. That's how much a bundle of furs weighed. Can you lift that many books?

2. Suppose you are in charge of getting supplies for a voyageurs' trip. They will be gone two weeks. There will be eight people in the group. On a piece of paper, list the supplies you will put in their canoes.

Chapter 4 Review

1. Which European country sent the first explorers to Wisconsin?

2. Who was the first white man in the Wisconsin region? Who was the second?

3. How did Jesuit priests help the settlement of Wisconsin?

4. Why did the French government send Marquette and Joliet to explore the Mississippi River?

5. What did Joliet and Marquette report about the land in Wisconsin?

6. Name two early settlements that started as French missions or trading posts.

7. Why did the trappers want beaver fur?

8. Name three interesting things about the voyageurs.

9. Which countries fought the French and Indian War?

10. Which country won the war and ruled Wisconsin?

Geography Tie-In

Geography is the study of a place. It includes the land, animals, and plants. Geography also is the people and where they build cities, what they do for a living, and where they move.

1. In this chapter, what waterways did you read about? What animal that lived in the rivers was important to our history?

2. Why did the explorers, missionaries, and trappers travel such a long way from Europe to America? How did this change life in Wisconsin forever?

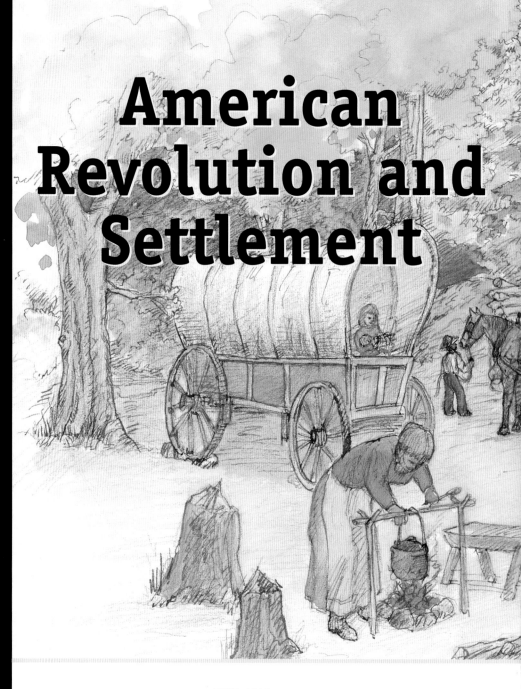

THE TIME
1775–1840

PEOPLE TO KNOW
John Jacob Astor
Black Hawk
Thomas Jefferson
James Johnson
Moses Meeker
George Washington
Laura Ingalls Wilder

PLACES TO LOCATE
Thirteen Colonies
Northwest Territory
Iowa
Nebraska
Green Bay
Mineral Point
Prairie du Chien
Pepin
Atlantic Ocean
Mississippi River
Bad Axe River

American Revolution and Settlement

1775–1783
American
Revolutionary War

1787
Northwest Ordinance

timeline of events

1770   1780   1790

1776
American colonies
declare independence
from Great Britain.

1783
Wisconsin becomes
part of the Northwest
Territory.

WORDS TO UNDERSTAND
independence
memorize
ore
Parliament
pioneer
recite
revolution
smelter
surrender
treaty

**Most of the early Wisconsin settlers lived in log cabins.
The people built the cabins with the trees they cut down.**

1800–1854
U.S. government makes land treaties
with Native Americans.

1825
Lead is discovered at Mineral Point.

1800	1810	1820	1830	1840

1832
Black Hawk War

Creation of America

PEOPLE TO KNOW
John Jacob Astor
Thomas Jefferson
James Johnson
Moses Meeker
George Washington

PLACES TO LOCATE
Thirteen Colonies
Northwest Territory
Green Bay
Prairie du Chien
Portage
Mineral Point
Atlantic Ocean

WORDS TO UNDERSTAND
independence
ore
Parliament
revolution
smelter
surrender

The British in America

As you read in the last chapter, the British gained control of Canada and all of the land east of the Mississippi River. Thirteen colonies on the East Coast already belonged to Great Britain. A colony is a settlement that is ruled by a country far away.

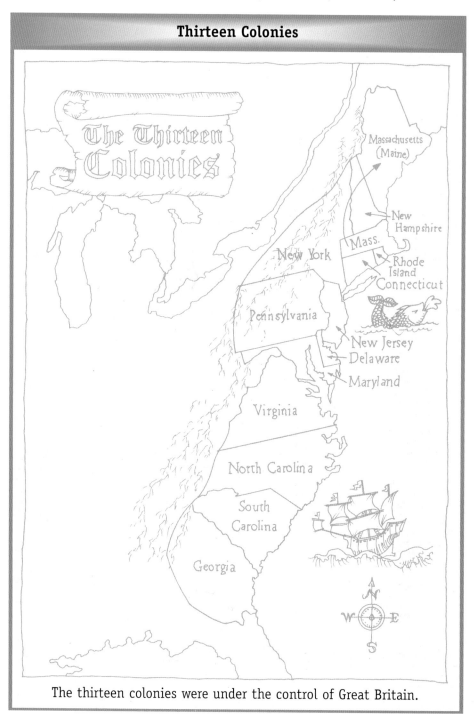

Thirteen Colonies

The thirteen colonies were under the control of Great Britain.

The Colonists Get Angry

People in the thirteen colonies were angry at Great Britain. Great Britain forced them to pay taxes even though they were not allowed to vote in *Parliament*. Parliament is the group in England that makes laws. The colonists said, "No taxation without representation!" That meant that they thought they should pay taxes only if they could help make the laws.

The American Revolution

The colonists declared their *independence* from the British. Thomas Jefferson was chosen to write a paper called the Declaration of Independence. He worked hard to find the best words to use. He wrote in a clear way. He explained that because the colonies had not been treated fairly, they were cutting all ties with Great Britain.

A *revolution* happens when people fight to replace one government with a different government.

In the Declaration of Independence, the colonists said that they would no longer be ruled by the British.

The colonists named themselves the United States of America. Of course, just saying they were free did not bring freedom. The new Americans had to fight a war to gain freedom from British rule.

Goodbye to British Rule

Across the Atlantic Ocean, the news that the colonies had decided to rebel made the British angry. British soldiers came to America to fight against the colonists. The British had more men than the colonists. They had a well-trained army and navy. The colonists were farmers, merchants, and other men who were not used to being soldiers.

After years of fighting, it looked like the Americans would lose the war. They didn't have enough soldiers. The soldiers did not have enough guns, warm clothes, or food. Then the Americans got the French to help them. The French supplied money, guns, ships, and soldiers. With the help of the French, the Americans won their independence.

The British had never expected to lose to the Americans. When the British *surrendered*, the British band played a song called "The World Turn'd Upside Down."

George Washington led the American army against the British.

Linking the past to the present

Do you and your family watch fireworks on the Fourth of July? Most Americans do. Americans are celebrating the day that the thirteen colonies declared their independence from Great Britain.

The Northwest Territory

After the Revolution, Wisconsin was part of the Northwest Territory. The Northwest Territory included the lands that would become the states of Wisconsin, Michigan, Illinois, Ohio, Indiana, and part of Minnesota.

The Northwest Ordinance

The Northwest Ordinance was a plan for how parts of the territory could become states. First, the huge piece of land would be divided into smaller territories. The smaller territories would then become states.

The Northwest Ordinance set rules for the new territory. Here are some of the rules:

- Slavery was not allowed.
- Land would be set aside for public schools.
- Settlers could practice any religion.

The Northwest Ordinance did not say anything about the American Indians already living on the land. This led to many problems between Indians and settlers.

Northwest Territory

The Northwest Territory is shown in white. The black lines show today's state boundaries. The land was not divided into states until later. Can you name the states?

What do you think?

Why do you think the writers of the Northwest Ordinance did not set aside land or make rules for the thousands of American Indians who already lived on the land?

The Growth of Wisconsin

After the Revolution, the French and Indians in Wisconsin continued to trade as they had for years. Slowly, however, other people began to find out about Wisconsin.

American Fur Traders and Soldiers

The first Americans to arrive in Wisconsin were fur traders and soldiers. Most fur traders worked for the American Fur Company. John Jacob Astor owned the company. He built all the trading posts. He hired many traders who were already in Wisconsin to work for him. They traded food, tools, and cloth to the Indians for furs.

Forts were built to help protect settlers and fur traders. Most of the forts were along trade routes. The most important trade route was the river route from Green Bay to Prairie du Chien. Forts were built in both places and at Portage, which was along the route.

The forts were small. Only a few hundred soldiers stayed in them. The men did not bring their families. Most of the men left after a few years. Other soldiers came to take their places.

Pioneers often settled near the forts for protection from Indians.
They cleared the land and started farming.

Lead Miners

Many of the first people to settle in Wisconsin from nearby states and other countries came to mine lead. Lead was used to make bullets, pipes, and paint.

James Johnson and Moses Meeker gave mining a great boost. These men opened mines and built *smelters*. Smelters were buildings with very hot ovens that melted *ore* into pure lead. Ore is rock that has minerals in it.

The center of the Wisconsin mining region was Mineral Point. The town was first called "Shake Rag." It got its name because the wives of the Cornish miners called their husbands to lunch by waving dishtowels. Cornwall is in England.

• Mineral Point

Shake Rag Street was lined with the homes of English miners.

The success of the mines brought more people to Wisconsin. Towns such as Platteville and Dodgeville grew quickly. Other mining towns with names such as Pin Hook, Nip and Tuck, and Big Red Dog also sprang up during the mining boom. Most of these towns were just shacks that disappeared as soon as the lead ran out.

The Badger State

Many early miners did not want to spend much time building homes. Instead, many dug holes in the ground. They covered up the openings with boards. The miners were called "badgers" because they dug holes in the earth just like badgers do.

Wisconsin is now called the Badger State.

Lesson 1 Memory Master

1. Why were the colonists upset with the British?
2. What was the name of the plan for parts of the Northwest Territory to become states?
3. Who were the first three groups of white people in Wisconsin?

Lesson 2

Indians and Settlers

PEOPLE TO KNOW
Black Hawk
Laura Ingalls Wilder

PLACES TO LOCATE
Iowa
Nebraska
Pepin
Mississippi River
Bad Axe River

WORDS TO UNDERSTAND
pioneer
memorize
treaty
recite

"The first white man we knew was a Frenchman. . . . He smoked his pipe with us, sang and danced with us . . . but he wanted to buy no land. The [Englishman] came next but never asked us to sell our country to him! Next came the [American] and he wished us to sell it *all* to him."
—Little Elk, Winnebago chief

A *pioneer* is one of the first people to do something. Why do we call settlers pioneers?

Gaining Control of the Land

At first, the American Indians were friendly to the new settlers. The Indians acted as guides for the settlers on the rivers and trails. But when more and more settlers came to Wisconsin, they began taking over the Indians' land.

The government made *treaties* with the Winnebago, Chippewa, Sauk, and Fox. A treaty is a written agreement signed by two groups. In the treaties, many Indian groups agreed to sell their land in Wisconsin and move across the Mississippi River to Iowa and Nebraska. They did not want to sell their land, but felt they had no choice. Often they didn't understand that they could not come back to their land.

The government bought land from the Indians for a low price. Then it sold the land to settlers. Settlers were able to buy large pieces of land at a low cost.

The Black Hawk War

Black Hawk, a Sauk Indian chief, was not happy that his people had agreed to sell their land. He said it wasn't fair. He thought the settlers should be the ones to have to leave. He led his people back across the Mississippi River to take back their land from the white settlers.

There was a terrible battle where the Bad Axe River flows into the Mississippi. The Native Americans were outnumbered. Black Hawk tried to surrender but was attacked again and again. Many of Black Hawk's people were killed.

The Black Hawk War was the last large war between Indians and settlers in Wisconsin. The United States government slowly gained control of most of the land.

Black Hawk was angry that the settlers had forced his people off their land.

Pioneers Come to the Northwest Territory

When boys and girls came to the Northwest Territory, they walked beside their family's covered wagon. The wagon was pulled by horses or oxen. Sometimes it was sunny, and it was fun to walk next to the animals, talk with new friends from other wagons, and race down to streams to cool off. Sometimes it rained, but they still had to keep going. At night, children slept inside the wagon or under it on a quilt.

The family wagon was crowded with trunks, furniture, oil lamps, quilts, bags of flour, dried meat, a spinning wheel, tools, and seeds. A shovel, water pail, and butter churn hung on the outside of the wagon. Cream churned itself into butter as wagons bumped along the road.

Dirt Roads

Early roads were only dirt trails with smashed-down grass. Most were old Indian trails. Travel was very slow.

Sometimes a road was so narrow the wagons could not pass through the trees. The men had to stop, get out of the wagon, and chop down trees. This could take hours. Sometimes a horse's hoof or a wagon wheel got stuck in mud.

Pioneers faced other problems. One woman wrote in her journal about crossing the Appalachian Mountains:

> *A dozen yoke of oxen were hitched to one wagon, and with hard pulling, they reached the top. Then men took the oxen down for the next wagon. Both men and beast could hardly walk they were so tired. After all the wagons were up, we took lunch on top of the mountains.*
>
> *Then we went down. Men hooked heavy chains behind the wagon. When the wagon started down, all the men held on for dear life and pulled back to keep the wagon from running down the mountain and crashing at the bottom.*
>
> *We were exhausted when we camped that night . . . for we had to walk all the way.*

—Mary Ackley

Biting, buzzing insects made life miserable for pioneers.

Pioneers used wagons to carry their belongings and for shelter on their way to their new homes.

Settlers had to clear the land before they could build their cabins.

"Our cabin had one room and a hole for a window and another one for a door. We put greased paper over the window. The cracks in the logs were chinked [filled in with mud] to keep the wind from whistling through."
—Jeanette Mitchell

The cabin was made with logs.

Traveling by Water

Whenever they could, the pioneers used the rivers as highways. It was a real adventure for a pioneer boy or girl to float downstream on a flatboat. Going by boat was easier than going across land. There were no rocky or bumpy roads. There were no trees to cut down or mud to get stuck in.

The boats were hard to steer, however, and sometimes they turned over in rough waters. Sometimes they got stuck in shallow water. Most of the time the ride was smooth. Children had plenty of time to watch the clouds or look for animals on the shore. Sometimes children could see Indian children who were watching them.

Pioneers came part of the way on flatboats. Even the animals got a ride.

Pioneer Life

Pioneer settlers usually started their farms near a fort or town. Everyone had a job to do on the family farm.

Pioneer Fathers

The father of the family bought the land. Then he began the hard job of clearing the trees. Most of the land in Wisconsin was covered with tall trees.

The father built a cabin with the logs. The cabin was small. Sometimes it had only one room. Later, he built a small barn for the animals and put up a fence around the pasture.

Pioneer Mothers

The mother of a pioneer family also had a lot of hard work to do. She cooked food on a wood-burning stove or in the fireplace. The fireplace also heated the cabin. She sewed all the clothes for her family.

The mother kept a small garden near the cabin. She planted vegetables and herbs used for cooking and making medicine. Each family grew all or most of its own food. The family also grew wheat or corn to sell.

Pioneer women made soap, dipped candles, and spun wool into yarn. At harvest time, women helped the men in the fields.

Pioneer Children

Children had important jobs to do, too. Children helped their mother cook the food. They cleaned up around the house. Older children carried in water from outside and cut wood. Younger children collected small branches and twigs for the fire in the cabin.

Everyone in a pioneer family worked very hard.

All the children helped their father plant seeds and pull weeds. They fed the chickens. Children also milked the cows. They took the cows out to the pasture during the day and brought them back into the barn at night.

Children slept in a loft under the roof of the house. To get up to the loft, they climbed a ladder. Their beds were made of sacks stuffed with straw and grass. After a while, the sacks smelled bad and were lumpy. The sacks had to be filled with clean straw.

Children went on errands for their parents. Sometimes this meant they traveled many miles all by themselves. Read this story of William, a nine-year-old boy. He lived on a farm with his family. William and his horse named Paddy had to take the wheat to town for grinding.

Father bought a black pony with the name of Paddy. He could carry three bushels of wheat and me on the top of it, or as many of the children as we could pile on.

It fell my lot to go to distant mills, and Paddy and I made many a mile of travel. At the mills, we had to wait our turn. Often we would have to leave our wheat and go after it another day.

The weather was fine, the roads were good, there were plenty of apples in the orchards and nuts in the woods by the way. They were always free!

Laura Ingalls Wilder

Little House in the Big Woods

Laura Ingalls Wilder is a famous author of children's books. She was born in Pepin, Wisconsin. She grew up in a small log cabin in the woods in Pepin. Wilder's books are called the *Little House* books.

Wilder wrote about living in a little log cabin in her book *Little House in the Big Woods*. She described how her family grew their own crops, fished, and hunted animals. She wrote about the hard times and the fun times she had growing up in the woods.

You can visit Pepin and see where Wilder grew up. In the summer, there are storytelling festivals. People tell stories and sing songs from the *Little House* books.

The "big woods" that Wilder knew as a child were cut down a long time ago. However, the trees are slowly being replaced. People have given money to buy trees to replace the ones that were cut down.

Read the words on the next page from *Little House in the Big Woods*. Would you like to grow up in a log cabin in the woods?

• Pepin

You can visit this model of Laura's childhood home in Pepin.

Once upon a time . . . a little girl lived in the Big Woods of Wisconsin, in a little gray house made of logs.

The great, dark trees of the Big Woods stood all around the house, and beyond them were other trees and beyond them were more trees. As far as a man could go north in a day, or a week, or a whole month, there was nothing but woods. There were no houses. There were no roads. There were no people. There were only trees and the wild animals who had their homes among them.

Wolves lived in the Big Woods, and bears, and huge wild cats. Muskrats and mink and otter lived by the streams. Foxes had dens in the hills and deer roamed everywhere.

To the east of the little log house, and to the west, there were miles upon miles of trees, and only a few little log houses scattered far apart in the edge of the Big Woods.

So far as the little girl could see, there was only the one little house where she lived with her Father and Mother, her sister Mary, and baby sister Carrie. A wagon track ran before the house, turning and twisting out of sight in the woods where the wild animals lived, but the little girl did not know where it went, nor what might be at the end of it.

The little girl was named Laura and she called her father, Pa, and her mother, Ma. In those days and in that place, children did not say Father and Mother, nor Mamma and Papa, as they do now.

—from *Little House in the Big Woods*, published by Harper & Row, 1932.

Laura and her sister Mary loved a game called mad dog.
Their father would run his fingers through his hair until it was messed up.
Then he got down on his hands and knees and growled and chased the girls.

Pioneer Schools

The school was made of logs. Inside, the floor was wood or just hard dirt. Children sat on long wooden benches. On cold days, a stove burned coal and wood. The children took turns bringing in wood to burn.

Children from every grade learned together in one room. Brothers and sisters sat in class together. Learning meant ***memorizing***. The teacher read a lesson to the students. Then the class repeated it over and over. One by one, the students stood up and *recited* the lesson from memory. If the child missed a word, or did not stand still while reciting, he or she had to do it over again until it was just right.

There was not much paper. Children wrote with chalk on small blackboards called slates. Sometimes, for practice, children wrote on smooth tree bark.

Children went to school about four months a year. The rest of the time they were too busy helping on the farm. Some lived too far away to go to school at all.

Be Good!

Pioneer schools were strict. Students had to sit up straight, be quiet, and always have their lessons ready. Students who did not pay attention had to stand in a corner or were hit with a thin wood rod. Sometimes students who did not behave had to write the same sentence hundreds of times.

Lesson 2 Memory Master

1. How did the government get Indian lands?
2. How did pioneers get to the Northwest Territory?
3. What kinds of work did fathers, mothers, and children do?
4. Who wrote the *Little House* books?

What's the point?

The United States was formed when the colonies won the Revolutionary War. Americans had fought a war against the British for the right to govern themselves and make their own laws.

After the American Revolution, people settled in the Northwest Territory. The new settlers built cabins and farmed. The government made treaties with the Indians to get land. Many Indians moved across the Mississippi River.

Activity

Research Your Town's History

Towns have histories. Investigate your town's history. When was the town founded? Why was it founded? Who were the first people to settle in the town? What is the oldest building?

You may discover surprising things. In River Falls, the middle school was built on the site of the oldest school in town. The land was given to the city to be used as a school many years ago.

Chapter 5 Review

1. What paper did the colonists write to declare their independence from the British?

2. After the American Revolution, Wisconsin became part of what territory?

3. Why did soldiers come to Wisconsin after the Revolution? Why were forts built?

4. What natural resource brought miners to Wisconsin?

5. Why is Wisconsin called the Badger State?

6. What war started because Indians were angry that they had sold their land?

7. What is a pioneer?

8. List three jobs that pioneer children did.

9. What is Laura Ingalls Wilder famous for?

10. List three things about pioneer schools that are different from your school.

McGuffey's Reader
The book taught children how to read.

Geography Tie-In

1. What things in nature (weather, landforms, animals, plants) made life easier for the early settlers?

2. Name four ways the settlers changed the natural environment.

THE TIME
1800-1890

PEOPLE TO KNOW
Edward Allis
Patrick Cudahy
Henry Dodge
James Doty
Margarethe Schurz
James Stout
Frederick Weyerhauser

PLACES TO LOCATE
Belgium
Canada
Denmark
England
Germany
Ireland
Norway
Poland
Sweden
Switzerland
Minnesota
New York
Washington, D.C.
Belmont
Janesville
La Crosse
Menomonie
Neenah-Menasha
New Glarus
Peshtigo
Superior
Watertown
Waukesha

Immigrants, Growth, and Statehood

timeline of events

| 1800 | 1810 | 1820 | 1830 |

1800s
Immigrants come to Wisconsin.

1825
Erie Canal
is completed.

1836
Wisconsin
Territory
is created.

chapter

6

WORDS TO UNDERSTAND
bellows
brewery
canal
economy
genealogy
grant
heritage
immigrant
industrialization
lefse
oppression
rosemaling
temporary
timberlands
tradition

**Thousands of children left their homes
in Europe to move to the United States.
Some of them settled in Wisconsin.**

1840   1850   1860   1870   1880   1890

1848
Wisconsin
becomes a state.

1850
First railroad in
Wisconsin is completed.

1871
Peshtigo
forest fire

1889
Bennet Law requires immigrant
children to attend school.
All classes must be taught in English.

Lesson 1

Immigrants

PEOPLE TO KNOW
Edward Allis
Patrick Cudahy
Margarethe Schurz

PLACES TO LOCATE
Canada
Belgium
Denmark
England
Germany
Ireland
Norway
Poland
Sweden
Switzerland
New York
New Glarus
Watertown
Hudson River
Lake Erie

WORDS TO UNDERSTAND
bellows
brewery
genealogy
heritage
immigrant
lefse
oppression
rosemaling
tradition

More People Come to Wisconsin

As you read in Chapter 5, more and more people moved to Wisconsin. They also came from eastern states and from Canada.

Many people came all the way from Europe. Many families came to farm.

Immigrants from Europe

Across the ocean in Europe, life was hard. Potatoes and other crops got diseases. There was not much good farmland. There were wars.

A person who leaves one country to settle in another is called an *immigrant*. Millions of immigrants came to the United States from Europe. Some of these people came to Wisconsin. Immigrants came to find good farmland. They wanted better work and more pay. Some people, especially Jewish people, came to find a place where they would be free to live their religion:

> *Papa said that it was no longer safe for a Jewish family . . . so we are going to America. . . . Papa and mama are busy selling most of our things. Mama told me and my little sister, Ana, to each pick one book and one toy to bring with us. Ana cried. She's only four. But I'm ten and must be brave, Mama says.*
>
> —Alvin Sandrovitch

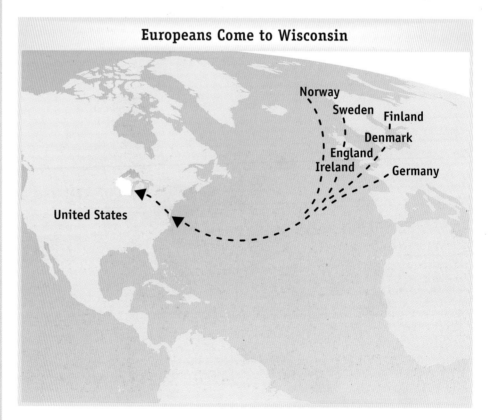

Europeans Come to Wisconsin

People came to America at different times. The Irish and Germans came before the Civil War. After the war, immigrants came from England, Norway, and Sweden. People from Belgium, Denmark, and Switzerland also came to Wisconsin. Later, many Polish people arrived.

The Journey to America

How did people get here? First, a family sold their land, house, and most of their things. Everything they took with them had to fit into a few trunks.

They had to find a ride in a cart to a seaport. Then they walked up a wooden ramp to get on a ship that would take them to the United States.

The trip across the Atlantic Ocean on a sailing ship was long and sometimes scary. For many weeks, the wind blew into the sail and pushed the wooden ship over the water. The boat rolled back and forth. Many children and their parents got seasick.

Here is what one person wrote about the trip:

> *All of us poor people had to go down through a hole to the bottom of the ship. There was a big dark room down there with rows of wooden shelves all around where we were going to sleep—the Italian, the German, the Polish, the Swede, the French —every kind. When the dinner bell rang we were all standing in line holding tin plates . . . waiting for soup and bread.*
>
> —Rosa Cristofero

The trip across the Atlantic was very long and hard.

"Imagine parting with all you love . . . selling the things dear to you . . . forced to go and make friends with strangers . . . suffering seasickness. How would you feel?"
—Mary Antin

Settling in America

Where Did They Settle?

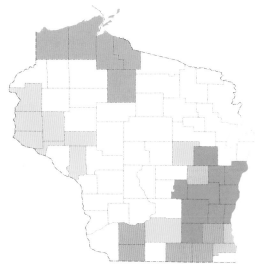

■ Norwegian, Swedish, and Danish
■ Finnish
■ German
■ British
■ British, Norwegian, Swedish, Danish, and German
■ British and German

Many immigrants first saw the United States at the harbor in New York. Others came to seaports all along the East Coast.

After passing an exam to make sure they did not have any diseases, immigrants went by train to Wisconsin. Buying train tickets and food was hard since most immigrants did not speak English. They could not read signs.

At the end of their long journey, the people who had money bought land. They usually settled in towns where people from their homeland already lived. In these places, immigrants could speak the language of their home country. They could keep their *traditions*.

You can get clues about the first settlers of a town by the names of the churches, the kinds of buildings, and the ethnic food served in restaurants. A group of Swiss immigrants founded a town called New Glarus. The town still has many traces of its Swiss *heritage*.

You can see Swiss-style buildings along the streets of New Glarus.

Immigrants had to wait in long lines at Ellis Island in New York. They were checked to see if they had any diseases. Some people were sent back to their homeland. Most of them, however, stayed in America.

▲ Photo of New Glarus by Kurt Leichtle

People Hear about Wisconsin

How did people on the East Coast and in Europe learn about the United States and Wisconsin? Why did people decide to move to Wisconsin?

Some people learned about Wisconsin from salesmen. The salesmen made money selling boat tickets to America. They also sold land.

Salesmen traveled to the East Coast and across the ocean to Europe to tell people to move to America. They talked about the beautiful valleys and rich farmland. They described green forests and beautiful lakes and rivers. The salesmen were sometimes called "soul stealers" because they talked people into leaving their homeland.

People also heard about Wisconsin from "American letters." People already living here mailed letters to their friends and family back home. Gunder Bondal wrote about Wisconsin's land in a letter to his family in Norway:

> *The land's richness is impossible for us to describe. . . . The land is not flat but rolling. It is layered with hills and valleys and mountains.*

Samuel Freeman wrote a book that told people to leave their troubles behind and come to Wisconsin:

> *We welcome you, for our land is broad, and we need your numbers. . . . We welcome you, for we know that, attracted by the fame of our country's freedom, many of you have come from **oppression** at home. . . . Cheer up and join America's glorious band.*

Germans

The largest group of Wisconsin immigrants came from Germany. Like many other people who came to Wisconsin, most of the Germans came to farm. The weather had been bad in Germany, and crops could not grow. Land prices were high. The promises of cheap land and jobs in the United States sounded very good.

Germans built farmhouses from timber.

At a German barn in Old World Wisconsin, these boys are looking at chickens through a barn door.

Once in America, German men and women started clubs, schools, and churches. The Turner Clubs were both social clubs and fitness centers. Today, Turner Clubs sponsor gymnastics. Germans opened their own schools, where classes were taught in German. The people spoke German in church services.

Germans helped shape Wisconsin's culture. German restaurants are scattered throughout Wisconsin. Bratwurst and other sausages are a common part of the American diet. Counties such as Dodge and Sauk still have very large German populations.

> "An endlessly fresh spirit surges through this land. Wherever you direct your gaze, something great can be seen developing."
> —Carl Shurz, a German immigrant

One author of this book is Kurt Leichtle. The Leichtles came from Germany.

One Girl's Story

Greta Steinmann looked out of her window onto the streets of Germany. She saw her two friends, Berta and Hanna, playing jump rope. She felt sad that she would be leaving soon.

"We will have a better life in America," Greta's father promised. "The land is good. There are more jobs."

For the next few weeks, Greta watched as her parents sold almost everything in their home. They packed trunks and bags with the most important things. Then the day finally came when it was time for Greta to say goodbye to all of her friends.

The next step was to travel across the Atlantic Ocean on a boat. The boat ride sounded exciting to Greta at first. But after many hours of being on the boat, Greta was bored. The boat was crowded and very cold. Big waves crashed against the boat. Everything was wet. Even the food was damp.

Weeks passed, and things got worse. People were sick. Greta's mother had a very bad cough, but there was no medicine.

Greta was sick of eating stale bread and cheese. She thought of the warm food her mother had made for her at home. She thought of Berta and Hanna. Tears rolled down her face. Greta wanted to go home.

Finally, Greta and her family stepped off the boat onto American land. Greta hoped that life would be better in America as her father had promised.

Linking the past to the present

Many people study their family's history. This is called *genealogy*. Has your family studied its past? Do you know where your family came from? When did they come to the United States?

Norwegians

Norwegians also came to Wisconsin. They packed their things in wooden trunks. The trunks were decorated with a style of fancy painting called *rosemaling*. The colors were bold and bright.

Struggling in a New Land

Immigrants helped build Wisconsin. Many worked as farmers. Some worked as lumberjacks and railroad builders. Some started small businesses.

Many immigrants lived in Milwaukee and other larger cities. In Milwaukee, many immigrants worked at the beer *breweries*. Patrick Cudahy hired immigrants to work in his meat-packing plant. Edward Allis hired immigrants to work in his factories.

Immigrants worked long hours. Sometimes they were paid less than other workers. Not everyone liked the immigrants. Some people thought that they would change the culture of the United States too much.

Some immigrants became discouraged and returned to their homelands. But many immigrants thought problems in America were not as bad as problems in the Old Country.

Education

People in Wisconsin wanted every child to be able to go to school for free. This had not happened in many places in the United States. Students in other places had to pay to go to school. If parents did not have enough money, their children could not go to school.

This *bellows* was used to fan the fire in a fireplace. A fire that got more air would burn hotter. This bellows is decorated with rosemaling.

Lefse is a thin round flatbread made from potato flour. Norwegians spread lefse with butter and jelly, folded them, and then ate them. Lefse was stored unfolded in the box.

What do you think these immigrant children are learning at school?

Government leaders in Wisconsin sold land to pay for education. The money paid teachers and bought books. Now every child could learn to read, write, and do math. The government even opened a school for deaf children in Janesville.

Immigrant children often had a hard time in school. Sometimes other children made fun of them because they could not speak English very well. Wisconsin passed a law. It said that all children had to go to school. All classes had to be taught in English.

Margarethe Schurz started the first kindergarten in America at Watertown for German children.

Linking the past to the present

How are public schools paid for today? Where does the money come from to pay all the people it takes to run a school?

How is this classroom different from classrooms today?

Immigrant Groups Today

Families still come to Wisconsin from many countries. They come from Mexico, Central America, Eastern Europe, and Asia. Where have immigrants in your community come from?

Where Did They Come From?

The largest numbers of people came from these countries:

1840–1860

Ireland
England
Wales
Scotland
Germany
Denmark
Norway
Sweden

1860–1900

Germany
Norway
Sweden
Denmark
Belgium
England
Ireland
Scotland
Canada

1900–1924

Poland
Eastern Europe
Central Europe
Russia
Italy

1924–1965

U.S. government
stops most immigration

1965–Present

Mexico
Central America
South America
Vietnam
Cambodia

"I can remember staring at the sea for hours, wondering what Milwaukee would be like. Going to America then was almost like going to the moon."
—Golda Meir

Lesson 1 Memory Master

1. What is an immigrant?
2. What are two ways that people on the East Coast and in Europe learned about Wisconsin?
3. What country did the largest group of immigrants in Wisconsin come from?

Lesson 2

Growth and Statehood

PEOPLE TO KNOW
Henry Dodge
James Doty
James Stout
Frederick Wyerhauser

PLACES TO LOCATE
Minnesota
Great Plains
Washington, D.C.
Belmont
Janesville
La Crosse
Menomonie
Neenah-Menasha
Peshtigo
Superior
Waukesha
Chippewa River
St. Croix River
Wisconsin River

TERMS TO UNDERSTAND
canal
economy
grant
industrialization
temporary
timberlands

The Wisconsin Territory

The Northwest Territory was divided up into smaller pieces of land. The Wisconsin Territory was one of the pieces. This was the next step toward statehood.

The first governor of the Wisconsin Territory was Henry Dodge. He chose Belmont to be the *temporary* capital.

▲ Photo by Wisconsin Division of Tourism

This is the first capitol building in Belmont.

The Thirtieth State

Many people wanted Wisconsin to become a state. Once Wisconsin became a state, it could receive more land from the government in Washington, D.C. The land could be sold. The money could be used to build roads, canals, and railroads. If Wisconsin became a state, leaders could vote for laws in Washington, D.C.

Before Wisconsin could become a state, however, its population had to reach a certain number. This was part of the reason salesmen worked hard to get people to move here.

The population of Wisconsin grew quickly after the Wisconsin Territory was created. The *economy* grew, too. Farming became more important than mining. Lumber also became a major industry.

Finally, there were enough people in the Wisconsin Territory for it to become a state. A state constitution was written. In 1848, Wisconsin became the thirtieth state of the United States of America.

A State Capital

Some people thought building a new capital city would be better than choosing a town that already existed. Every town wanted to be the capital city. There would be more business in a capital city.

It was finally decided that a new town would be built to be the capital. The town of Madison was built. Madison soon had roads, homes, businesses, and government buildings.

• Madison

The Story of the Two "Ds"

In the years before Wisconsin became a state, its history was affected by the two "Ds"—Henry Dodge and James Doty. Both men became Wisconsin governors. Both served in Congress. In some ways, they looked like each other. They were both over six feet tall. Neither had a beard. They held their heads high and walked proudly. But they were also very different.

Henry Dodge was known as a young man with fearless honesty. He had a temper, however, that sometimes got him into trouble. Though he could read and write, he had not gone to school much. He was a war hero. He came to Wisconsin and made a place for himself in the rough world of lead mining.

Dodge often shocked people. He dressed in rugged clothes and usually carried a knife. He used bad language. He once scared a hotel maid by leaving his large knife under the pillow. Dodge had a reputation for using his strength and will to get his way.

James Doty went to school and became a lawyer at the age of twenty. He was always polite, and he dressed well. But people did not always trust him. Doty was not always honest.

Doty received the credit for pushing Wisconsin to become a territory. Later, when Wisconsin became a state, he was elected as a senator. He went to Washington, D.C., to help make laws for the whole country.

A Time of Change

Wisconsin and the United States changed from a land of farmers and small businesses to a place with many large factories. This was called *industrialization*. More people worked for big, powerful companies. More work was done by machines.

The Lumber Industry

The first big businesses in Wisconsin were lumber companies. Frederick Weyerhauser, James Stout, and other men got *timberlands* from the U.S. government. Then they hired lumberjacks to cut Wisconsin's pine trees.

Wisconsin lumber helped build a growing nation. Some of the boards helped to build houses for workers in cities to the east. Farmers on the Great Plains also used wood from Wisconsin.

Each winter, the lumberjacks went into the woods to cut huge trees. Men lived at camps in the woods. Each morning, the cook woke up the lumberjacks by yelling, "Daylight in the swamp."

After breakfast, the men worked all day out in the cold. Logging was hard, dangerous work. Many loggers were hurt by falling trees. Some men fell into the rivers during the log drives.

Lumberjacks sawed down huge trees and cut off the branches. Horses and oxen pulled the heavy logs to the edges of streams and rivers.

The Largest Lumber Company

James Stout was an owner of a Wisconsin lumber business. Knapp, Stout and Company became the largest lumber company in the United States. Stout used some of the money that he made to start a school in Menomonie. Both men and women went to the school. The Stout school is now part of the University of Wisconsin.

Photo by Sunny Walter

Trees were cleared from the land. The logs were used to build houses in the growing cities in Wisconsin and in other places.

Lumberjacks pushed the logs into the river. Hundreds of logs floated down the river to the sawmills. The trip down the river was called a "log drive." At the sawmills, powerful saws cut the logs into flat boards. Most Wisconsin logs traveled this way until train tracks were laid.

Sometimes the logs were caught in a logjam. The lumberjacks had to use log poles, or even dynamite, to try to get them apart. One jam on the Chippewa River was fifteen miles long.

Driving Logs on the River

Huge log jams often blocked rivers.

The St. Croix, Wisconsin, and Chippewa Rivers were used for log drives.

Lumbering made the owners of the lumber companies rich. Some people worried about cutting too many trees. Soon most of the great pine forests were gone. Bare land covered northern Wisconsin. Most people, however, still saw logging as an important business.

Fire!

Fire was a danger in the forests. The Peshtigo fire burned the land around the town of Peshtigo. Flames reached high into the air. There was no way to put the fire out. It burned itself out. More than a thousand people died.

Years later, Wisconsin created a system to protect the state's forests. Fire towers were built. They can still be seen in many of Wisconsin's state forests.

"I saw nothing but flames; houses, trees, and the air itself were on fire."
—Peshtigo man

From Towns to Cities

Wisconsin had been a state of farms and small towns. The towns grew into larger cities. Most of the big companies were in Milwaukee. German, Irish, and Polish immigrants lived in Milwaukee. The city had many large factories. The Edward P. Allis Company made steam engines and sawmill equipment. Later, it made engines that made electricity. There were also many breweries in Milwaukee.

Wisconsin also had smaller cities. Superior, in the north, was a transportation center. La Crosse had farm machinery factories. Neenah-Menasha made paper.

Canals

How did people get to Wisconsin? Traveling on trails and roads was slow. They traveled on the water whenever they could. Traveling on water was much easier and faster than traveling on land. A *canal* is a waterway made by people. Canals connect rivers and lakes. Thousands of men dug out dirt to make a place for the water to go. Horses and wagons carried away the dirt.

Travelers left New York on boats and floated on the Erie Canal all the way to Lake Erie. Then they went across the Great Lakes to Wisconsin. More and more people from the East came to Wisconsin after the Erie Canal was built.

Building canals was very hard work. Workers dug a trench 40 feet down and 25 feet across.

▲ Photo by John Ivanko

Mules pulled the canal boats along a towpath.

There were several small canals in Wisconsin. Canal boats were small and very narrow. They were pulled through the canals by mules. The mules walked beside the canals on a towpath.

Traveling on a canal boat was an adventure. Boats carried about fifteen people. People brought their own food and sometimes even live animals. Would you have liked to take your dog or goat with you on a canal boat? The boats stopped along the banks of the river for the night. Sometimes people camped out in tents.

Once travelers reached the shores of Wisconsin, they used wagons or carts pulled by horses to travel to cities. Roads were often dusty or muddy, depending on the weather. Roads had tree stumps sticking up in the middle of them and lots of rocks. The ride was very bumpy.

"In the warm summer nights, the canal swarmed with laughing, shouting boys. They jumped from the bank and splashed in the water."
—William Dean Howells

Steamboats

The steamboat was invented to make travel by water faster. Coal made a hot fire that heated water. When the water boiled, the steam pressed against parts of the engine and made them turn. The turning paddle wheel made the boat go fast. The best part was that you didn't have to wait for the wind to push the boat.

Many people were afraid when they first heard the puffing engines and the whirling paddle wheels. They were used to quiet sailboats.

Steamships brought immigrants to America. Steamships traveled much faster than sailing ships.

Railroads

The first train tracks in Wisconsin went from Milwaukee to Waukesha. There were few railroads anywhere in the United States at that time.

The government helped build railroads by giving railroad companies land on both sides of the route. This was called a land *grant*. The railroads could sell part of the land and use the money to pay workers.

The Wisconsin Central, the Soo Line, and the Burlington and Northern were important railroad lines. They hauled lumber products, grain, and minerals.

Superior became a major shipping port. Trains brought iron ore from northern Minnesota. The trains stopped on top of the wooden docks, a door opened at the bottom of each car, and the ore spilled out. Later, the ore was loaded onto ships and taken to steel mills in the East.

Lesson 2 Memory Master

1. Why did people want Wisconsin to become a state?
2. What were the first big businesses in Wisconsin?
3. How did the government help build railroads?

What's the point?

During the 1800s, Wisconsin changed. It became more like it is today. Farming and small businesses had been important. Then companies got even bigger. Towns became large cities.

Immigrants moved to Wisconsin from Europe. The people wanted to leave their problems behind. They wanted a better life. They saw Wisconsin as a land of opportunity.

Wisconsin finally became a state. The people of Wisconsin looked to the future with hope.

Activity

What Should I Take?

Pretend you are moving to another country. You must travel like the immigrants did 100 years ago. You can't pack much. You will be riding on a boat with hundreds of strangers. There is hardly room for you, and not much room for your things. You must carry everything that you bring with you.

What will you choose to take? Imagine that you have a grocery bag. You can take only those things that will fit into the bag. Make a list of what you will bring. Explain why you chose each item.

Chapter 6 Review

1. What are two reasons people left Europe to come to the United States?

2. What was the town that a group of Swiss immigrants started?

3. What did most German settlers do to earn money?

4. Name two ways German immigrants left their mark on Wisconsin.

5. What city was built to be the capital of Wisconsin?

6. In what year did Wisconsin become the thirtieth state?

7. What is a canal?

8. How did steamboats make traveling on water faster?

9. Why were railroads important?

10. Name three important railroad lines in Wisconsin.

Geography Tie-In

1. On a world map in your room, find all of the places on the immigrant chart on page 89. From what countries have recent immigrants come? What continents are these countries on?

2. Use library books or the Internet to learn about one of the countries immigrants came from. What kind of place is it? What is the land like? How do the people live?

THE TIME
1850–1865

PEOPLE TO KNOW
John Wilkes Booth
Sherman Booth
Alvan Bovay
Joshua Glover
Cordelia Harvey
Abraham Lincoln
Douglas MacArthur
Arthur McArthur
Alexander Randall
Vinnie Ream
Carl Schurz

PLACES TO LOCATE
Africa
Canada
Germany
Illinois
Michigan
Washington, D.C.
Madison
Milwaukee
Ripon

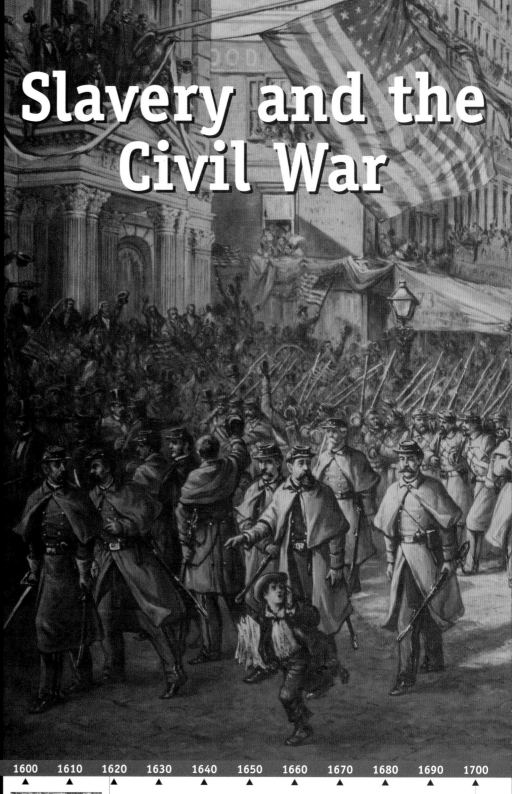

Slavery and the Civil War

timeline of events

1600	1610	1620	1630	1640	1650	1660	1670	1680	1690	1700

1619
First slaves
are brought to
North America.

7

WORDS TO UNDERSTAND
abolitionist
advocate
assassinate
border states
Confederacy
conflict
enlist
plantation
sculptor
secede
shell
Union

Union soldiers went off to fight in the Civil War.

1860
Abraham
Lincoln is elected
president.

1865
Lincoln
is assassi-
nated.

| 1710 | 1720 | 1730 | 1740 | 1750 | 1760 | 1770 | 1780 | 1790 | 1800 | 1810 | 1820 | 1830 | 1840 | 1850 | 1860 |

1700s
Some slaves worked in Wisconsin mines
and as house servants.

1787
Northwest Ordinance
outlaws slavery in the
Northwest Territory.

1854
Republican Party is
formed in Wisconsin.

1861–1865
The Civil War

The Slave Trade

The slave trade had been going on in America for hundreds of years. Black men, women, and children were captured in African villages. African and European slave traders chained up the Africans and loaded them onto ships. Slave traders took them across the Atlantic Ocean.

People were packed closely together in the bottom of the ship. During the trip, the slaves did not get much food or water. There was no fresh air. Many of them got sick and died on the journey.

When the ships landed, the traders sold the Africans who were still alive. People bought slaves to work on farms, in factories, or in mines. The French brought slaves to Wisconsin to work in the lead mines.

Slavery ended in Wisconsin with the passage of the Northwest Ordinance. You learned about it in Chapter 5. The rules said there could be no slavery in the Northwest Territory. However, slavery was not against the law in the southern states.

Slaves were kidnapped from their homes in Africa, chained together, and forced onto ships that took them far away.

The Hard Life of a Slave

Some slave owners treated their slaves well. They treated them like trusted servants. Other masters were very cruel. They didn't think of slaves as people. Many slaves lived through each day with fear.

Some slaves lived on large sugar or cotton *plantations* in the South. From sunrise to sunset, they worked for the master. Slaves worked all day in the hot sun. The slaves dreamed of Sunday, the one day of the week they were allowed to rest.

A plantation was a farm in the South. Some plantations were very large. Plantations grew cotton, tobacco, sugar, or rice.

The overseer watched from his horse as slaves worked.

"My brothers and sisters were bid off first . . . while my mother held me by the hand. My mother pushed through the crowd to the spot where [her new master] was standing. She fell at his feet, [begging] him to buy at least one of her little ones."
—Josiah Henson

At slave auctions, slaves were sold to the highest bidders. Mothers and fathers were often separated from their children. They were sold to different masters. Sometimes brothers and sisters never saw each other again.

What do you think?
Why is it important to remember the terrible, sad parts of history as well as the good parts?

Learning to Read

Slaves were not allowed to read or write. Slave owners were afraid that if slaves could read and write, they would write notes to each other. They might make plans to escape. They might read maps and plan how to get away. Slave children could not go to school anyway. They had to work.

Still, some slaves learned to read in secret. Being able to read was a way of saying to the masters, "You can never own my mind."

Slave Culture

Slaves spoke a mixture of African languages and English. They told stories about their homeland to their children. They sang songs about God, work, freedom, and escape. Their music was the beginning of modern jazz music.

Sherman Booth

Sherman Booth lived in Milwaukee. He worked for an *abolitionist* newspaper. Abolitionists demanded that all slaves be freed.

Once Booth led a mob of men to free Joshua Glover, an escaped slave, who was being held in a Milwaukee jail. Glover's owner had traveled from Missouri to Milwaukee to claim Glover and return him to slavery.

Sherman Booth vowed to prevent Glover from being returned to Missouri. Booth rode his horse through the streets of Milwaukee, calling on people to help free Glover. Booth led a mob to overrun the jail. They took Glover from the jail and sent him to Canada.

Booth was arrested. Booth fought in court for six years, until the charges were finally dropped. His actions stirred the antislavery feelings in Wisconsin.

The Underground Railroad

Life was so hard for the slaves that many tried to escape. They used the "Underground Railroad." The Underground Railroad was not a train at all. It was not even under the ground. It was many secret routes that slaves used to escape to the North. The word "underground" meant it was a secret.

Mostly men ran away, but some women and children also escaped to freedom.

Sometimes slaves did travel by railroad, but they usually went by boat, horse, and on foot. They usually traveled during the night so they wouldn't be seen.

There were people all over the North and South who thought slavery was wrong. They helped slaves escape. Strangers met boats and took slaves to homes where they could get food. Sometimes the strangers drove carts with slaves hidden under a layer of straw.

Everything about the Underground Railroad had to be kept secret. The people who helped the slaves along the way used special code words and signals. Slaves were called "railway workers." Houses where slaves hid were called "stations." "Conductors" led slaves to the next station.

For some slaves, the trip on the Underground Railroad took months or even years. For others, it took only two or three days. It all depended on how far they had to travel and how much help they got.

The Underground Railroad in Wisconsin

Most people in Wisconsin were against slavery. They wanted to help slaves find freedom. The Underground Railroad had many routes and stations here.

The Milton House was a station on the way to Madison. Slaves were taken into the basement. Then they walked through a tunnel to a secret room. Many runaway slaves ate, slept, and hid at the Milton House.

Most slaves who came into Wisconsin went on to Canada. Others stayed here or went to work in Minnesota.

What do you think?

Slaves had a terrible life. Why do you think white people were once allowed to own slaves?

Some masters hunted down their runaway slaves. The masters offered a reward to the person who caught the slave. The slaves were punished and sometimes killed.

Milton House

The Republican Party

People in government don't always think the same way. People who share the same ideas form groups called political parties. Today, the two main parties are the Democrats and the Republicans.

The Republican Party was formed to fight slavery. Some of the meetings were held in the town of Ripon in an old schoolhouse. Wisconsin is often said to be the birthplace of the Republican Party. But people in Illinois and Michigan also claim that the party was started in their state.

Ripon •

Alvan Bovay led the Republican Party meetings in Ripon. The Republicans wanted to run against the Democrats in the next election. Men like Bovay believed that the Democrats supported slavery because the Democratic Party was very popular in the South.

The Republicans sent a message to *The New York Tribune*. The message announced the beginning of the Republican Party. People all over the nation read the newspaper. People in other places started Republican groups.

Lesson 1 Memory Master

1. What continent did most slaves come from?
2. What was the name of the secret routes that slaves used to escape to freedom?
3. Who helped organize the Republican Party in Wisconsin?

The first meetings of the Republican Party were held in this schoolhouse in Ripon.

A Nation Divided

What if half of the classes in your school said they no longer wanted to be part of your school? What if they said they were leaving because the school rules did not let them do what they wanted to do?

During the Civil War, states in our country did this very thing. These states did not like the rules the government had made. They decided that they wanted to be a separate country. They *seceded*, or left, the Union.

When people in a country disagree so much that they fight against each other, it is called a civil war. In the American Civil War, states fought against other states. Friends fought against friends. Sometimes brothers fought against brothers.

States' Rights

There had been a lot of *conflict* between the states for a long time. The main issue concerned what a state could and could not do.

People in the South thought states should have more power than the United States government. They did not want the national government telling them what to do.

People in the North thought the national government should continue to make laws for all the states. They thought it was important to have laws for people living in all parts of America.

Slavery

Another major problem was slavery. Southern plantation owners said they had to have slave labor. Many slaves were needed to work on the huge cotton, tobacco, rice, and sugar plantations.

Many people in the North thought slavery was wrong. In the North, many people worked in factories and mines. Men also built canals and railroad tracks. There were farms in the North, but there were not as many farms as in the South. The farms in the North were smaller than the ones in the South. Farmers did not need slaves to work on the smaller farms.

Who Would Have the Most Power in Congress?

Slavery became a huge issue when new states joined the United States. Since each state sent two senators to make laws in Washington, the free states thought slavery would never end if the slave states had the most voting power in government.

The conflict over slavery was about right and wrong. But it was also about who would have the most power—the North or the South.

Lesson **2**

The Civil War

PEOPLE TO KNOW
John Wilkes Booth
Cordelia Harvey
Abraham Lincoln
Douglas MacArthur
Arthur McArthur
Alexander Randall
Vinnie Ream
Carl Schurz

PLACES TO LOCATE
Germany
northern states
southern states
Washington, D.C.
Madison
Milwaukee

WORDS TO UNDERSTAND
advocate
assassinate
border states
Confederacy
conflict
enlist
sculptor
secede
shell
Union

The Civil War Begins

Abraham Lincoln was elected president of the United States right before the Civil War began.

Lincoln said he would not stop slavery in the South. But he said he would not allow slavery in new states. This made people in the South mad. They wanted to make their own laws about slavery. They wanted more slave states in the West.

Soon all of the southern states left the United States. They formed their own country. They called it the Confederate States of America, or the *Confederacy*.

The northern states were called the *Union*. There were four slave states that did not leave the Union. These states were called *border states*.

President Lincoln's goal during the Civil War was to keep the United States united—no matter what.

President Lincoln said, "A house divided against itself cannot stand." What do you think he meant by that?

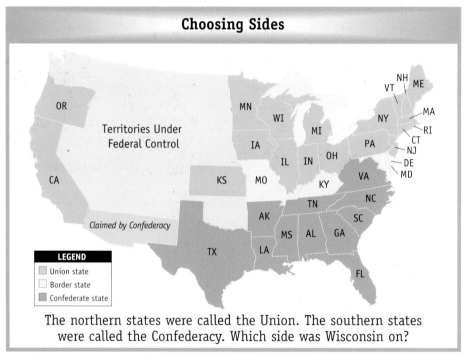

Choosing Sides

OR

Territories Under Federal Control

CA

Claimed by Confederacy

MN
WI
IA
KS
MO
TX
LA
AK
MS AL GA
TN
KY
IL IN OH
MI
PA
VA
NC
SC
FL
NY
NH
VT
ME
MA
RI
CT
NJ
DE
MD

LEGEND
☐ Union state
☐ Border state
☐ Confederate state

The northern states were called the Union. The southern states were called the Confederacy. Which side was Wisconsin on?

Old Abe

Many generals of the Union army thought Wisconsin soldiers were among the best fighters. Two groups were very famous—the Iron Brigade and the Eagle Regiment. The Eagle Regiment got their name from their mascot, Old Abe.

Old Abe was a bald eagle. He was with the soldiers in many battles. He perched on cannons and flew over the battle sites, screaming his war cry. After the war was over, he returned to Wisconsin with the soldiers.

Old Abe lived at the Capitol Building until he died.

President Lincoln met with Union soldiers after one of the worst battles of the Civil War.

Most of Wisconsin's soldiers were teenage boys between the ages of nineteen and twenty.

Wisconsin's Role in the Civil War

President Lincoln asked Wisconsin's governor to send men to help the Union. Governor Alexander Randall sent many more men than Lincoln had asked for. People in Wisconsin felt strongly that the Union had to be saved. But as the war went on, it became more difficult to get people to volunteer to be soldiers. People were less certain that the North would win.

Most Wisconsin soldiers trained in Madison to fight in the army. A training camp there was named in honor of Governor Randall.

Linking the past to the present

Today, the University of Wisconsin Badgers play football at Camp Randall Stadium. The stadium is on the site of the Civil War training camp. Have you been to Camp Randall Stadium?

A War Hero

The most honored Wisconsin war hero was Arthur McArthur. He was a teenager from Milwaukee. He was eighteen years old when he went to war. He won many awards for his bravery in battle.

Later, McArthur's son, Douglas MacArthur, was one of the United States' most important leaders in World War II. He changed the spelling of his family's last name.

WISCONSIN
P·O·R·T·R·A·I·T

Carl Schurz

Carl Schurz came from Germany. He wanted to live in a free country. He settled in Wisconsin. He joined the Republican Party because it was against slavery.

Schurz worked hard in Abraham Lincoln's campaign for president. Schurz was able to reach German voters since he spoke German. Schurz was also a general during the Civil War. After the war, he helped Congress with its plan to rebuild the nation.

After the slaves were freed, Schurz was a strong *advocate* of voting rights for African Americans. He continued to work the rest of his life for freedom and equal rights for all people.

Women and Children in the War

Wisconsin women and children helped the war effort. Women and children took care of the family farm while the men went off to fight in the war. Women went to work in mills and factories. Other women set up hospitals for soldiers. Cordelia Harvey set up a hospital in Wisconsin for wounded and sick men. Some women felt they were not doing enough to help. They dressed as men and became soldiers or spies.

Most soldiers were at least eighteen years old, but some younger boys also went to war. In the North, young boys played the drum in the army. Many boys lied about their age so they could fight in the war. Later, the Confederacy passed a law allowing boys under eighteen to *enlist* in the army. Some boys as young as eleven fought in the battles.

Many boys became homesick and scared during the war. They watched as men were wounded or killed. Elisha Stockwell wrote what he was feeling:

This ten-year-old boy was a drummer boy in the Union army.

> As we lay there and the **shells** were flying over us, my thoughts went back to my home, and I thought what a foolish boy I was to run away and get into such a mess as I was in.

After the war, the government changed its rules. The Civil War was the last time young boys fought for our country.

The End of the Civil War

After four long years of war, thousands of men were dead. Thousands were badly wounded. Many had lost arms or legs. One in every seven Wisconsin soldiers died in the Civil War. Finally, the South surrendered.

Confederate General Robert E. Lee surrendered to Union General Ulysses S. Grant.

The Death of President Lincoln

President Lincoln was *assassinated* only days after the war ended. The president and his wife were watching a play at Ford's Theater in Washington, D.C. A man who had been a Confederate shot Lincoln.

People in Wisconsin and around the country were very sad. President Lincoln had led the country through the Civil War. He had fought for freedom for all people.

John Wilkes Booth shot President Lincoln at a theater in Washington, D.C.

End of Slavery

About six months after the Civil War ended, the Thirteenth Amendment to the Constitution was passed. It outlawed slavery everywhere in the United States.

Lesson 2 Memory Master

1. List two reasons the southern states seceded from the Union.
2. Who was president during the Civil War?
3. Which side won the Civil War?

What's the point?

The northern states and the southern states argued over who was going to have the most power—the national government or state governments. They also fought over slavery. There did not seem to be a good way to make both sides happy. A Civil War broke out. Many Wisconsin men went to fight in the war. Luckily, there were no battles fought in Wisconsin.

The Civil War was a hard time for our country. Abraham Lincoln did his best to keep the states together. Finally, the Union won the war. The country came back together. The slaves were free.

WISCONSIN
P·O·R·T·R·A·I·T

Vinnie Ream

Vinnie Ream was born in Madison. Her family later moved to Washington, D.C. During the Civil War, she visited the studio of a *sculptor*. Sculptors make statues.

Vinnie Ream began studying how to make statues. Within a year, she was making statues of people for government offices. She told people that she wanted to make a statue of Abraham Lincoln. Lincoln heard about this and invited her to the White House to work on her statue.

After Lincoln was murdered, Congress wanted to have a marble statue of Lincoln made. They interviewed many sculptors. They finally chose Vinnie Ream to make the statue. Since she was only eighteen years old, many people thought she was too young.

People liked Ream's statues. She found more work. She earned her living making statues of famous Civil War heroes.

Activity

Cause and Effect

Whenever we do something, something else happens. When we enter a dark room and flip on the light switch, the room is filled with light. This is called cause and effect. The cause is flipping on the light switch. The effect is that the room is filled with light.

Life is filled with cause-and-effect relationships. So is history.

CAUSE: Action that happens first and causes something else to happen

EFFECT: What happens because of the action

Look at each pair of sentences below. On a separate piece of paper, write "C" for the cause and "E" for the effect.

EXAMPLE:

  _C_   The northern and southern states could not agree.

  _E_   The southern states seceded from the Union.

1. ___ Farmers in the South planted huge fields of cotton and tobacco.

   ___ Southern farmers needed many field workers.

2. ___ Some of the slaves made it to freedom.

   ___ Brave people risked their lives to escape from slavery.

3. ___ A master punished a slave girl.

   ___ A slave girl was caught learning to read.

4. ___ Lincoln loved to read books and newspapers.

   ___ Lincoln learned many different things.

5. ___ The southern states left the Union.

   ___ Lincoln was elected president.

6. ___ Women were not allowed to join the army.

   ___ Some women dressed up as men and joined the army.

Chapter 7 Review

1. Name two crops that were grown on plantations in the South.

2. What Underground Railroad "station" was located in Wisconsin?

3. Where were the meetings of the Republican Party held in Wisconsin?

4. The southern states declared themselves independent. They _____ from the Union.

5. The states disagreed about states' rights, slavery, and _____ .

6. What were the four slave states that did not leave the Union called?

7. Why did Carl Schurz join the Republican Party?

8. List two ways women helped during the Civil War.

9. Did the Union or Confederacy win the Civil War?

10. Who assassinated President Lincoln?

Geography Tie-In

Look at the map on page 106.

• Was Wisconsin a Union or a Confederate state? Was slavery allowed here?

• What kinds of states surrounded Wisconsin? Were they Union states, border states, or Confederate states?

▶ Photo by John Ivanko

Wisconsin's soldiers fought for the Union.

THE TIME
1870–1920

PEOPLE TO KNOW
Alexander Graham Bell
J.W. Carhart
Henry Ford
Belle Case La Follette
Robert M. La Follette
Woodrow Wilson

PLACES TO LOCATE
Austria-Hungary
England
France
Germany
Italy
Russia
Michigan
Appleton
Green Bay
Kenosha
Madison
Milwaukee
Oshkosh
Racine
Superior
Brule River

A New Century of Progress

timeline of events

1870

1880

1873
J.W. Cahart builds the first
steam-powered carriage.

1879
The light
bulb is
invented.

1880s
First motion
pictures are made.

1886
Appleton has the first
electric trolley system
in the United States.

Housing in many cities was run down and dirty.
People wanted to make things better.

chapter

8

WORDS TO UNDERSTAND
century
generator
governor
Industrial Revolution
kerosene
labor union
mass production
neutral
Progressive
sewage
strike
veteran
war bond

1890   1900   1910   1920

1892
The
automobile
is invented.

1895
Radio is
invented.

1901
Robert M.
La Follette
is elected
governor of
Wisconsin.

1903
First Harley-
Davidson
motorcycles
are sold.

1907
One in twelve
homes in Wisconsin
has electricity.

1914–1918
World War I

1917
The United
States enters
World War I.

A New Century

People look forward to the beginning of a new *century*. A new century is a chance for a fresh start. That's how many people in Wisconsin thought about the year 1900. It was the first year of the twentieth century. Men and women wanted to fix problems in Wisconsin. They wanted to build a better America.

Cities and Industries Grow

Towns and cities were growing in Wisconsin. Many people were moving from farms to towns and cities. More and more immigrants came to Wisconsin.

Many people went to work in factories. Machines had been invented that could make things faster than people could make them by hand. This time period is called the *Industrial Revolution*.

Wisconsin factories made all kinds of products. Men, women, and children worked in factories that made clothing and shoes. Some people went to stores to buy clothes just like we do today. Before that, all clothes were made at home. Workers at other factories canned fruits and vegetables, or turned grain into flour. Papermaking was also a large industry. Trains carried goods to other places to be sold.

A canning factory was a noisy place. Canned food lasts a long time without going bad.

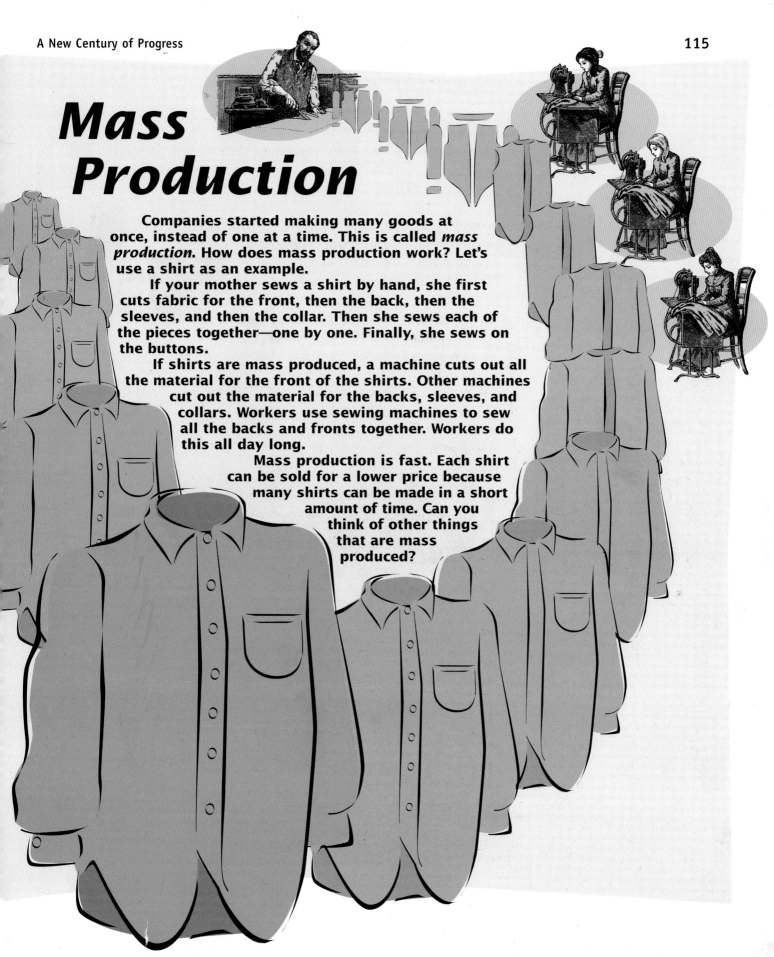

Mass Production

Companies started making many goods at once, instead of one at a time. This is called *mass production*. How does mass production work? Let's use a shirt as an example.

If your mother sews a shirt by hand, she first cuts fabric for the front, then the back, then the sleeves, and then the collar. Then she sews each of the pieces together—one by one. Finally, she sews on the buttons.

If shirts are mass produced, a machine cuts out all the material for the front of the shirts. Other machines cut out the material for the backs, sleeves, and collars. Workers use sewing machines to sew all the backs and fronts together. Workers do this all day long.

Mass production is fast. Each shirt can be sold for a lower price because many shirts can be made in a short amount of time. Can you think of other things that are mass produced?

Working in Factories

The growth of cities and industries caused many problems. Business owners made a lot of money, but they paid very low wages to workers. The men, women, and children who worked in factories were poor. The whole family worked to make enough money for rent and food.

A factory worker's life was very hard. There were not many laws that said how factory workers should be treated. Many factory owners did not care about their workers. They did not give them a safe place to work.

All the machines made the factories hot and noisy. Sometimes the machines hurt workers. If a machine cut off a worker's hand, the worker was fired because he or she could no longer work. Bosses pushed workers to work faster. People worked twelve to fourteen hours a day.

Child Labor

Children as young as seven years old worked in factories with adults. Children gave the money they earned to their families.

Boys and girls who worked in factories could not go to school. Outside the cities, some children of farm workers did not go to school either.

Children worked long, hard hours. Can you tell what these children are doing?

Workers Join Together

Factory workers began to think about how to make things better. One worker could not change things alone. If a worker complained, he or she was fired. There were so many other people looking for jobs that the owners could easily find someone else to work.

Workers joined together to fight for change. They formed *labor unions*. Unions often went on *strike*. Workers refused to go back to work until their demands were met. Strikes often led to violence.

Workers in Wisconsin went on strike because they wanted higher wages and shorter working days. Many people were working twelve hours each day. They wanted to work eight hours for the same pay. They said they couldn't live on any less money.

Shoemakers organized a labor union in Milwaukee. It was called the Knights of St. Crispin. Leaders from the Knights of St. Crispin helped organize a strike.

The Bay View strike happened when workers from many different factories joined together to try to get the government to make working conditions better. Business owners did not want to make changes.

Fights broke out between the police and the strikers. The strikers lost and had to return to work. Both the workers and owners were left with many bad feelings.

Workers went on strike to try to make working conditions better.

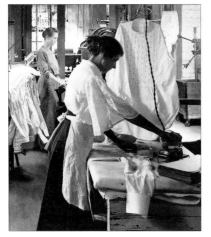

These women are at work ironing shirts.

Linking the past and the present

In the early 1900s, many factory workers in the United States were women. Before this time, most women had not worked outside of their homes.

Today, women work at many kinds of jobs. Women are doctors, teachers, lawyers, truck drivers, engineers, business managers, repair people, electricians, and computer programmers. Many women work at home, taking care of their children and their homes.

Progressive Reform

What were some of the problems Wisconsin faced in 1900? Most of the problems were in the cities. Cities had grown quickly. Many cities were crowded and dirty. The streets were not paved. More policemen and firemen were needed. Streets needed to be cleaned and garbage needed to be collected. More schools were needed.

Many people lived in crowded, dirty apartments and houses. Diseases spread quickly. Garbage and *sewage* from open sewers leaked into the water supply. Pollution from industries made the air dirty. Contaminated milk was a major cause of diseases.

Industry gave people jobs and made things people needed. But factories made the air and water dirty. Black soot clung to buildings. Smoke hid the sun in some parts of the cities.

Linking the past and the present

What problems in your city need to be fixed? What things are better today than they used to be?

Factories made the air dirty.

The families in this building shared one water faucet in the hall.

Water was often not clean. People got sick from it.

"There is death in our drink."
—*Daily News* reporter

Wisconsin Progressives

People who wanted to fix problems were called *Progressives*. Progressives had great hopes for the future.

Wisconsin Progressives were led by a man name Robert La Follette. In 1900, La Follette was elected *governor* of Wisconsin. A governor is the leader of a state. La Follette and the Progressives fixed many problems in Wisconsin.

Wisconsin Progressives built new roads. They built new schools. They set up a state park system to protect the beautiful land in our state. They planted trees to replace the trees that had been cut down by lumber companies.

Progressives passed laws making factories safer places to work. They passed laws that protected children from working long hours. They passed laws so companies would have to pay the doctor bills for people who were hurt at work. They also passed minimum wage laws. The laws said that people could not be paid less than a certain amount for every hour they worked.

Progressive Laws Make Things Better

Across the United States, Progressives passed laws that helped make life better. They passed laws so that:

- workers could not be fired for joining a labor union.
- mines had to have safety rules.
- young children could not work in mines.
- workers hurt on the job would still get paid.
- bosses had to pay their workers no less than a certain amount of money.
- companies could not pollute the air and water.
- more policemen and firemen would work in the cities.
- city streets would be paved.
- cities would collect garbage.

- cities would put in sewer systems for indoor bathrooms. Before this, people used outhouses.

- milk sold in stores would be clean and fresh.

Big Business

The railroad and logging industries were very powerful. But they often were not honest. They cheated to get their way. They wanted to control the government. They paid people in government to vote the way they wanted them to. They did not pay their taxes.

The Progressives wanted to make sure powerful businesses paid their taxes, and they wanted to fix the government. In the old system, political parties held big meetings to choose people to run for office. Big businesses often controlled these meetings. La Follette passed the primary election law. This law said that all members of a political party could choose the men and women who would run for office.

WISCONSIN P·O·R·T·R·A·I·T

Belle La Follette and Robert M. La Follette

Robert La Follette grew up in a log cabin in Wisconsin. He wanted to be an actor. While in college, La Follette was told that he was not tall enough to be an actor. He became a lawyer and later went into politics instead.

After serving as governor, La Follette became a U.S. senator. Many of the Progressive reforms he had passed in Wisconsin were passed nationwide. He ran for president, but he did not win.

La Follette was very thankful for his wife, Belle. Belle helped him in his career. She even wrote many of his speeches. Robert called his wife his "wisest and best counselor." He talked about the years "when we were governor."

Belle was the first woman to graduate with a law degree from the University of Wisconsin. She was a strong supporter of women's voting rights. She also wanted African Americans to have the same rights as white people.

Robert La Follette's sons followed in his footsteps. Robert Jr. represented Wisconsin in Congress. Philip served as governor of Wisconsin.

Lesson 1 Memory Master

1. What was the Industrial Revolution?
2. To try to get their demands met, workers joined _____ _____.
3. List four things that Progressives wanted to fix.
4. Who led the Progressives in Wisconsin?

Inventions Make Life Easier

Many things that we take for granted today did not exist 100 years ago. People did not have televisions or computers. Most people did not have cars or telephones. Life was very different.

Electricity

A little over a hundred years ago, people cooked food and heated their houses by filling a stove with coal or wood. Then they had to light a fire. Today, people use gas or electric heat.

To get light, people filled a lamp with an oil called *kerosene*. Today, people flip a switch to turn on a light.

Electric *generators* were one of the most important new inventions. Generators are machines that make electricity. They make electric lights possible. New machines that used electricity were invented. There were electric washing machines, irons, stoves, refrigerators, and vacuum cleaners.

Streetcars no longer had to be pulled by horses. They could run along electric wires. Cities like Milwaukee, Racine, and Kenosha grew because people could live farther away from the city's center. Electric trolleys took people downtown and then took them back home. Appleton had the first electric trolley system in the United States.

GOOD LUCK

People used to use hand powered washing machines. Today, we use electric washing machines.

Telephones

People used to have to walk across town to talk to someone. Alexander Graham Bell's invention—the telephone—made it easier for people to communicate. It took quite a while before all homes and businesses in Wisconsin had telephones.

Linking the past and the present

Bell's invention led to other inventions. Today, your computer can use your phone line to send e-mail anywhere in the world.

Lesson 2

Inventions and World War I

PEOPLE TO KNOW
Alexander Graham Bell
J.W. Carhart
Henry Ford
Woodrow Wilson

PLACES TO LOCATE
Austria-Hungary
England
France
Germany
Italy
Russia
Michigan
Green Bay
Kenosha
Madison
Milwaukee
Racine
Superior
Oshkosh
Brule River

WORDS TO UNDERSTAND
generator
kerosene
neutral
veteran
war bond

Sewer Systems

People used to get water from a well or spring. They carried the heavy water to the house in buckets. This took a lot of time. Sometimes the water was not clean. People's outdoor toilets drained straight into the ground. Sometimes human waste got into the well water that people drank. People died from terrible diseases.

Sewer systems were built to collect waste water. Sewers carried dirty water to places away from houses and apartment buildings.

The whole family liked to listen to the radio together.

Radio

By 1930, many people who lived in cities and some who lived in *rural* areas had radios. In the evenings, people sat in their livingrooms and listened to the radio. Voices seemed to come out of the air. People could hear music, news, and special shows called "radio theatre." These were programs that told stories. In the fall, fans could listen to broadcasts of the University of Wisconsin football games.

Movies

People went to a lot of movies. The first films were silent, with no talking or music. Some fancy theaters, like the Palace in Superior, had organists who played during the film. A movie ticket cost twenty-five cents for adults and ten cents for children.

Automobiles

Many families bought their first car during the 1920s. Before that time, only rich people had enough money to buy large "touring cars." But for $400, many families could now buy a car. Cars gave people freedom to go wherever they wanted to go.

Contest Winner!

J.W. Carhart of Racine built the first "horseless carriage" that used steam. He called the carriage the "Spark." It could travel four miles per hour. The people of Wisconsin were very excited about Carhart's invention.

The state government decided to hold a contest. $10,000 was to be awarded to the person who could build a horseless carriage that was "a cheap . . . substitute to the use of horses and other animals on the highway."

To pick the winner, a race was held from Green Bay to Madison. Only two people showed up to race their steam-powered carriages. One person was from Green Bay. The other was from Oshkosh. The carriage from Green Bay broke down on the way to Madison. The carriage from Oshkosh made it to Madison. The winning carriage had traveled six miles per hour.

The winning car from Oshkosh cost $1,000 to build. The judges said the car was not affordable. The inventor won only $5,000 instead of $10,000.

The first cars came in only a few styles. Henry Ford owned the factory that made Ford cars in Michigan. He joked that people could have any color of car they wanted as long as it was black.

Roads were just paths made of dirt. When the weather was dry, people choked on the dust. When it rained, cars got stuck in the dirt that had turned to mud.

Wisconsin started to build better roads. One of the first paved roads was in northern Wisconsin. The road was between Superior, where President Calvin Coolidge had his "Summer White House," and the Brule River, where he went fishing. No one wanted the president's car to get stuck in the mud or covered with dust.

The Ford Motor Company was located in Michigan. Workers used the world's first assembly line to make cars.

People often made fun of the early cars. When they saw a car in trouble, they yelled, "Get a horse."

World War I

The people of Wisconsin were making progress. They had cleaner water. Workers were paid more. Many people could afford electric lights and telephones. Some had cars. Then a terrible war started across the ocean in Europe. The fighting involved so many countries that it was called the Great War. Years later, it became known as World War I.

The Great War involved all of the major countries of the world. On one side, there were the Central Powers. The Central Powers included Germany and Austria-Hungary. On the other side, there were the Allies. The Allied Powers included England, France, Italy, and Russia.

Joining the Allies

At the start of the Great War, the United States tried to stay *neutral*. America did not want to take sides. America continued to buy goods from both sides and sell goods to both sides. President Woodrow Wilson wanted to keep the United States out of the war.

Not everyone believed that the United States should fight in the war. Most of Wisconsin's congressmen did not want America to go to war. Robert La Follette did not want America to go to war.

But something happened that made the United States join the Allies. Germany used submarines to sink American ships that were taking goods to England and France. America entered the war.

Wisconsin Helps Fight the War

Many men from Wisconsin went to fight in Europe. Some died in the war. Many farms in Europe were destroyed. American soldiers and people in Europe needed food. Farmers at home grew more crops. Boys from the cities helped farmers harvest their crops. Food grown in Wisconsin was shipped overseas.

People at home helped by buying *war bonds*. They paid money for government bonds. This gave the government money to pay for the war. After the war, people traded in their war bonds for money.

Wisconsin companies started making supplies soldiers needed. Companies made things like uniforms, army boots, and guns.

The War Ends

The fighting finally stopped. People in Wisconsin and across the nation celebrated. Towns held parades to honor the soldiers. Soldiers marched through the streets as people cheered. November 11, the day the fighting stopped, is now celebrated as Veteran's Day. A *veteran* is a person who has fought in a war.

Posters urged everyone to help in the war effort. What does Uncle Sam—in his red, white, and blue—stand for?

Germans in Wisconsin

There were many German people living in Wisconsin. Since Germany was one of the countries America was fighting against, German Americans tried to prove their loyalty to the United States. They bought a lot of war bonds. Some German Americans even changed their last names to sound American. For example, Germans who had the last name "Braun" might change their name to "Brown."

Women Help in the War

Women from Wisconsin helped the war effort. Women cooked meals without wheat or meat, so those foods could be sent to Europe. They worked as nurses in hospitals. They served food to soldiers. Women made hospital supplies at Red Cross centers. They made clothes and bandages for soldiers. Many women also went to work in factories that made war supplies.

Girl Scouts collected peach pits for the war effort. The pits were turned into charcoal. Charcoal was used in gas masks to filter out poisonous gas.

Some women worked as nurses.

What do you think?

World War I was known as "the war to end all wars." Has this turned out to be true?

Lesson 2 Memory Master

1. Name three new inventions that made life easier.
2. Why did the United States decide to fight in World War I?
3. How did Wisconsin help the country during the war?

What's the point?

The beginning of the twentieth century was a time of great change. Progressives in Wisconsin and throughout the United States passed laws to try to make things better. They passed laws to clean up the cities, fix the government, and make working conditions better.

Life changed during World War I. People from small towns moved into cities. More women went to work outside the home. Many people did not return to the way of life they had before the war.

When peace returned, the factories that had made things like guns and army boots made other things people wanted. Everyone looked forward to better days.

Activity

Catalogs Now and Then

Shopping was difficult for people who lived in small towns. When people lived a long way from stores, they often shopped by mail. All kinds of products were listed in catalogs. People mailed in their orders and money for things they wanted. Here are some items that were sold in early catalogs:

- clothes for men, women, and children
- oil lamps
- ice boxes
- supplies for horses
- wagon wheels
- plows

Make a list of items you have seen for sale in catalogs today. Have your parents ever ordered anything?

What is Sears, Roebuck & Company selling on this page of their catalog?

Perry, Dame & Company sold clothes.

Do these shoes look like shoes people wear today?

Chapter 8 Review

1. What is a century?

2. What is mass production?

3. List three problems that the growth of cities and industries caused.

4. What is a strike?

5. List four things Progressives wanted to fix in Wisconsin.

6. How did big businesses control the government?

7. How did electric trolleys help cities grow?

8. What was the "Spark"?

9. Why did Woodrow Wilson want to keep the United States out of World War I?

10. What holiday is celebrated on November 11?

Geography Tie-In

Progressives worked to clean up cities. They built new schools. They built new roads and paved old roads. They built sewer systems.

Make a list of ways your city or neighborhood has changed. Were the changes good for people? Were they good for animals? Talk with your class about how you can make your community a better place to live.

Apartment buildings got so hot in the summer that families went up on the roof to sleep outside. Can you see the factories in the city?

THE TIME
1920–2000

Good Times and Bad Times

timeline of events

1920	1930	1940	1950

1920s
The Roaring Twenties
The Great Migration

1930s
The Great Depression

1941
December 7
The Japanese bomb Pearl Harbor, Hawaii. The U.S. enters World War II.

1920
Women win the right to vote.

1919–1933
Prohibition

1939–1945
World War II

chapter 9

Black and white students usually went to separate schools. This was called segregation. Schools for black students were not as good as other schools. To end school segregation, black students were bussed to white schools. These people in Milwaukee wanted all children to have better schools, but they did not want to send them on a long bus ride across town.

Photo by *Milwaukee Journal Sentinel*

1960   1970   1980   1990   2000

1950–1953
Korean War

1960s
Civil Rights
Movement

1963–1975
Vietnam War

1991
Persian Gulf
War

2000
A new century
begins.

The Roaring Twenties

People wanted to forget World War I. Factories stopped making war materials. Factories started making things for people at home. There was enough work for everyone. People wanted to buy all of the things they saw in store windows.

This time is called the "Roaring Twenties" because of all the new things people did to have fun. There were goldfish-swallowing contests and all-night dances. Sports were popular, too. The Green Bay Packers played their first season in 1921. They won ten out of eleven games.

Like other Americans, people in Wisconsin started listening to a new type of music called jazz. Jazz started in African American cities in the South, especially New Orleans. The music spread to cities in Wisconsin.

People enjoyed new kinds of dances in the 1920s.

Women started working at jobs that had only been open to men. Women cut their hair short and wore shorter dresses. Women who did this were called "flappers." Sometimes this shocked other people.

The Great Migration

Starting in the 1920s, many African Americans moved from farms and towns in the South to cities in the North. They moved to Milwaukee and other cities in Wisconsin. This was called the Great Migration.

Black people left the South for several reasons. States there had taken away their right to vote. Southern whites made laws that black people had to follow. The laws were called "Jim Crow" laws. Jim Crow laws were used to keep white people separate from black people.

African American students had to attend schools just for blacks. They had to sit in the back of buses. Public places, like libraries and parks, were *segregated*. African Americans could not go into the "white sections" of public places. Water fountains had signs above them that said "white only" or "colored only." Movie theaters had "colored only" seats. Even cemeteries were segregated.

In the North, jobs in industry paid well. Black people could vote. Schools were better. But many whites did not want to live or work with blacks. People would not give blacks an equal chance because of their skin color.

There were still not many African American people in Wisconsin. Most of the black people in Wisconsin lived in Milwaukee and they could only live in the worst part of town. Schools were segregated. There were no segregation laws, but rules and understandings kept African Americans segregated.

The Ku Klux Klan in Wisconsin

A group called the Ku Klux Klan attacked Catholics, Jews, immigrants, and especially African Americans. Klan members wore white hoods to hide their faces. They did not want people to know who they were.

A newspaper in Madison published an advertisement for people to join the Ku Klux Klan. The ad read,

> Wanted . . . men of ability between the ages of 25 and 40.
> Must be 100% Americans.

A few years later, however, the Ku Klux Klan in Wisconsin had almost disappeared. Most people thought the Klan was very un-American. They did not like the bad things it did.

KKK members wore white hoods to scare people.

Harry Houdini

Harry Houdini was born in Hungary. He moved to Appleton with his family when he was four years old. Houdini soon became a trapeze performer in the circus.

Houdini was also interested in magic. He read about Robert Houdin, who was a great magician. He learned that in the French language, when the letter "i" is added to a word, it means "like." That is how he got his name—"Houdini." His real name was Ehrich Weiss, but he wanted to be "like Houdin" someday.

People liked to watch Houdini's escape tricks. He could free himself from ropes, handcuffs, boxes that had been nailed shut, and locked jail cells. He made many movies. In the movies, he always got free.

These women were "bootleggers." They secretly made whisky and beer to sell.

Prohibition

During this time, the United States made it *illegal* to make or sell alcohol. This was called Prohibition because the government *prohibited*, or stopped, people from making and selling alcohol. Wisconsin had lots of breweries that had to close down. This hurt business in Wisconsin. People who supported Prohibition believed that the state and the country would be better off if liquor was not sold.

When Prohibition ended, most people in Wisconsin were happy. When news reached Milwaukee that beer would be legal again, people celebrated with parades and parties. They even sent some Milwaukee beer to President Franklin Roosevelt in Washington, D.C.

Women Gain the Right to Vote

Women have not always had the right to vote. At the beginning of the twentieth century, many women in Wisconsin and the rest of the United States fought for women's *suffrage.*

Women marched in the streets. They carried signs that said women should have the right to vote. They made speeches. Mithilde Anneke, Laura Ross, and Olympia Brown worked for women's suffrage in Wisconsin. Anneke worked for a newspaper. Ross was a doctor, and Brown was a minister.

Finally, the 19th Amendment to the Constitution was passed. It gave women the right to vote.

Women fought hard to gain the right to vote.

The Great Depression

A *depression* is a time when many people are out of work. They don't make enough money to take care of their families. People want to work, but they can't find jobs.

The depression of the 1930s was the worst depression the United States has ever known. That is why it is called the Great Depression.

Factories in Milwaukee, Green Bay, Racine, and Kenosha shut down. More than half of the workers in Wisconsin lost their jobs.

Many farmers in Wisconsin lost all of their money. Prices were so low for crops and dairy products that farmers were not making any money. Farmers across the country were also suffering from a serious *drought*. There was not enough water for crops.

Governor Philip La Follette did what he could to make things easier for people in Wisconsin. He hired men to improve old roads and build new ones. He set up a program that gave money to people who had lost their jobs. He helped farmers pay their bills.

People did what they could to survive. Slums like this one in Milwaukee were common in the cities.

How People Survived

Many families lost their homes. Some people moved in with relatives. Some people lived under bridges or made shelters out of scrap wood or metal. People tried to help each other as much as they could.

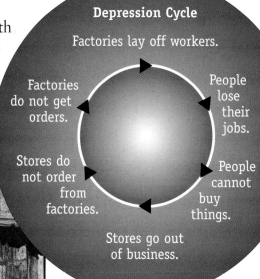

Depression Cycle

Factories lay off workers.

People lose their jobs.

People cannot buy things.

Stores go out of business.

Stores do not order from factories.

Factories do not get orders.

Many families were very poor during the depression. Eleven members of the Bettinger family lived in this small cabin.

134

Milwaukee and other cities around the country had breadlines and soup kitchens where people could get free food.

Men sold apples on street corners to earn money. Families grew gardens in their backyards. They mended old clothes again and again to try to make them last. They put cardboard in the bottom of their shoes to cover up the holes.

We wore clothes made out of material from old clothes. We put cardboard in our shoes, and when they wore out we wore any shoes we could get our feet into. They hardly ever fit.

The New Deal

People began to wonder if the depression would ever end. They were worried that life would just get worse and worse. But President Franklin Roosevelt had a plan. He called his plan the New Deal.

Roosevelt started projects to create jobs. The government hired people to do all sorts of work. People built dams, fixed highways, built new government buildings and schools, and made parks.

"I pledge you, I pledge myself, to a new deal for the American people."
—President Franklin Roosevelt

▲ Photo by Dorthea Lange

President Roosevelt had polio, a disease that left many children and adults unable to walk. Roosevelt worked hard for the country even though he couldn't stand up without help.

The government made jobs during the depression. These workers are making a brick street.

Governor Philip La Follette and Senator Robert La Follette Jr. tried to help the people of Wisconsin. Governor La Follette suggested several programs to help the poor. Senator La Follete Jr. supported the New Deal programs.

Linking the past to the present

One of the New Deal programs helped older Americans. It was called Social Security. Part of the money people earned went to retired people. When the workers retired, they would also get social security money. Social security is still working today.

Lesson 1 Memory Master

1. Name three things that people did for fun during the Roaring Twenties.
2. What was the Great Migration? Why did it happen?
3. What happens during a depression?
4. What did President Roosevelt do to help end the depression?

World War II

Like Americans, many people in other countries were suffering through the depression. President Roosevelt and the New Deal helped Americans get through those difficult years. Not all countries were so lucky.

In some places, *dictators* took over the government. A dictator is a ruler who has all of the power. Adolf Hitler was the dictator of Germany. Italy also had a dictator. Dictators stopped holding elections. They killed people who were against them. In Japan, the army took over the government.

The dictators of these countries wanted to take over other countries. When the German army invaded Poland, all of Europe went to war. On the other side of the world, Japan invaded China.

Attack at Pearl Harbor!

The United States did not get involved in the war for two years. Americans tried to stay *neutral*. Then something terrible happened in Hawaii.

One morning in December, Japanese airplanes dropped bombs on the American navy base in Pearl Harbor, Hawaii. The bombs destroyed ships and planes and killed people.

The next day, the United States declared war on Japan. Once again, we were at war. We were fighting against Germany, Italy, and Japan. On our side were England, France, and Russia.

The United States entered the war when Japan bombed Pearl Harbor.

Wisconsin Does Its Part

Many Wisconsin men and women served in the armed forces. They were ordinary people from small towns and big cities. Many died in the war.

General Douglas MacArthur led the American forces. He had lived in Milwaukee for a while. The Japanese captured many Wisconsin soldiers. MacArthur directed the attack that set them and other prisoners free.

Wisconsin farmers made cheese and grew crops for the soldiers fighting the war. Industries made guns, trucks, and ships. Factories made clothes and blankets for soldiers. Factories also made guns, trucks, and ships.

Richard Bong was a pilot during the war from the small town of Popular, Wisconsin. Bong was awarded the Congressional Medal of Honor, the highest military award. His statue stands today in Popular.

•Popular

Iwo Jima

The Iwo Jima World War II statue is made of bronze. Six marines are raising the American flag on top of a rocky hill on the tiny island of Iwo Jima in the Pacific Ocean. Japan owns the land today.

James Bradley, from Antigo, Wisconsin, wrote a book called *Flags of Our Fathers*. The book follows the lives of the six teenage boys who fought in the war and raised the flag. Bradley's father grew up in Appleton. He was one of the boys who raised the flag. Some of the young men died on the island.

James Bradley wrote his book so people would know what war is really like. He wanted them to know that war is not a game. It is a horrible thing.

Six young men raised the American flag on the island of Iwo Jima. Bradley is third from the left, with both hands on the pole.

Golda Meir

Golda Meir was born to a Jewish family in Russia. She moved with her family from Russia to Milwaukee when she was seven years old.

Meir went to a teachers' college in Milwaukee after high school. She then taught in public schools in Milwaukee.

After a few years of teaching, she moved with her husband to Palestine. Palestine is now called Israel. She became a political leader in Palestine. She held many important positions in the government there.

Meir said, "I never did anything alone. Whatever we did, we did it by working together."

The End of World War II

After years of fighting and millions of deaths the United States and its allies defeated Germany. Japan fought on for several more months. Then Japan surrendered. World War II was finally over.

The Holocaust

Millions of people died during World War II. But that number does not include the deaths of six million Jews and six million other people in Europe. They didn't lose their lives in battle. They were murdered by Hitler's soldiers.

Adolf Hitler believed that Germans were better than other kinds of people. He believed the world would be better without different kinds of people. He especially hated the Jews.

First, Hitler took away Jewish people's rights. Jews were forced out of their jobs. Some Jews left Germany, but most stayed. They thought that because they were German they would be safe. They were wrong.

Later, Hitler's troops rounded up all the Jewish people they could find. Jews were forced into railroad cars and sent to *concentration camps*. These were prison camps. Men and women were separated. Many never saw each other again.

At the camps, there was hardly anything to eat. The people were forced to do hard labor. People who were too old, too young, or too weak to work were killed.

When the war ended, American soldiers went to free the prisoners in concentration camps. They were *horrified* at what they saw. The soldiers described the people as walking skeletons.

Jews had to wear a yellow star so everyone knew they were Jews. Only one of the children from this family—the girl on the bottom right—survived the war.

Civil Rights Movement

After World War II, black leaders began to speak out against the treatment of black people. *Civil rights* marches were held in many cities in Wisconsin. Civil rights are the rights that belong to every citizen. People marched at the state capital and at several universities. There were many marches in Milwaukee. Milwaukee was one of the most segregated cities in the United States.

African Americans lived in the oldest buildings in a segregated neighborhood west of the Milwaukee River. They had moved to Wisconsin because things were better here than in many other states. But still there were not many jobs for African Americans. Many companies would not hire them. Most of the jobs available to blacks were low paying.

African Americans usually went to all-black schools and whites to all-white schools in Milwaukee. Father James Groppi fought to end this segregation. He was a white Catholic priest from Bay View. He led marches and protests. It took a long time for things to get better.

> **"Darkness cannot drive out darkness; only light can do that. Hate cannot drive out hate; only love can do that."**
> —Martin Luther King Jr.

Hundreds and sometimes even thousands of people protested for civil rights.

Do you think the person who made this poster was for or against the ERA?

The Women's Movement

Women also fought for equal rights during this time. Groups of women joined together to try to get women's wages equal to men's, make it so companies could not give some jobs only to men, and elect more women to government offices.

Many people wanted to pass the Equal Rights Amendment (ERA). They said it would give women equal rights under the law. Other men and women did not like the ERA. They worried that women would have to fight in wars with men. They thought it was better for families when women stayed home and took care of their homes and children. The vote was close, but not enough states voted to add the ERA to the U.S. Constitution.

Other Wars

Since the end of World War II, people from Wisconsin have fought in other wars. These wars have included the Korean War, the Vietnam War, and the Persian Gulf War.

The Vietnam War was the longest war our country has ever fought. It lasted over ten years. American troops went overseas to fight in Vietnam. They tried to keep the communists from taking over the government. *Communism* is a form of government in which people cannot own property or choose where they will live. They do not get to vote for their leaders. They can't choose a religion. They don't have the freedoms that we have.

People held many *protests* against the Vietnam War. Sometimes the National Guard was called to make sure the protests stayed peaceful.

The Vietnam War was the most unpopular war in American history. Many people protested against the Vietnam War. Other Americans thought it was important to stop communism from spreading to other countries.

What do you think?

Do you think America should help other countries fight their wars? Or should we fight only to protect our country? Ask adults you know what they think.

Activity

Searching for Answers—Your Own Interview

Interview an older person who lived during the Great Depression or World War II.

Before the interview, get together with other students in your class and make a list of questions you would like to ask. Here are a few ideas:

- Do you remember the Great Depression?

- Was anyone in your family out of work?

- What things were hard to do without much money?

- Do you remember World War II?

- How old were you when the war started?

- Did you know anyone who fought in the armed forces? Where did the person fight?

- How were things different after the war ended?

Wisconsin's People Today

People in Wisconsin celebrated the beginning of the twenty-first century with fireworks and parties. They looked back at the history of our state and the world. They also looked forward to our future.

Each of us is a part of history. We are all important to our family, state, and country. When you clean up your neighborhood, you help protect our environment. When you collect food for people who are hungry, you are helping to solve the problem of poverty. When you welcome someone from a different place, you are making the American dream real. Who you are and what you do today is the history of tomorrow!

Who Are We?

Total Population: 5,363,675

Other
0.5%

American Indian
1.0%

Asian
1.5%

Hispanic
3.5%

African American
5.5%

White
88%

1. A census is a count of people in a place. How many people lived in Wisconsin in 2000 when this census was taken?
2. How many different groups did people say they belonged to?
3. Which group was the smallest (besides "other")?
4. What countries might Asians (or their ancestors) have come from?
5. What group is the second largest?
6. What group is the third largest?
7. What people might have said they were "other" in the census count?
8. What are some important ways all the people are alike?

SOURCE: 2000 U.S. Census Report

Lesson 2 Memory Master

1. What happened to bring the United States into World War II?
2. What was the Holocaust?
3. Which groups of people tried to win equal rights?
4. What other wars has the United States fought since World War II?
5. What was the longest war?

What's the point?

The twentieth century was a time of great change. There were good times and bad times. People struggled to overcome the Great Depression. There were many wars that changed people's lives all over the world. African Americans and women fought for equality.

The struggles of the last century have continued into the twenty-first century. Americans and people around the world continue to solve problems to make our world a better place.

Chapter 9 Review

1. What group attacked African Americans, Catholics, Jews, and immigrants?

2. What liquor law caused many problems in Wisconsin?

3. What important right did women win during the 1920s?

4. What was life like during the Great Depression?

5. How did President Roosevelt put people back to work?

6. What happened at Pearl Harbor?

7. What did people from Wisconsin do to help the country during World War II?

8. What changes did African Americans want?

9. What changes did some women want?

10. How can Wisconsin people make this a great place to live?

Geography Tie-In

On a map of the world, find the countries that fought on the same side as the United States during World War II. These countries were called the Allied Powers. Then find the countries that fought against the United States. These countries were called the Central Powers.

Government for
All of Us

WORDS TO UNDERSTAND
amendment
bill
candidate
district
federal
independent
jury
legislator
local
nominate
ordinance
political party
representative
republic
sentence
veto

People in Wisconsin must follow
the laws of both the government
of the United States and the state
government of Wisconsin.

Photo by Wisconsin Division of Tourism

Government for the Nation

On July 4, 1776, the American colonies declared their independence from England. They set up a new nation called the United States of America. They wanted their country to be a *republic*. This meant there would be no kings or queens. The people would elect leaders to make laws.

The people fought a war with England. Finally, after many years of war, America was a free country.

The first national government of the United States joined the states into a "league of friendship." The states kept most of their power. They could write state constitutions and raise taxes. The national government could not tax the people.

What do you think?

Can you imagine living in a country where every state made all their laws? It would be like fifty separate countries.

James Madison, George Washington, and other men met to write the Constitution.

New Problems

Soon the young nation had many problems. The country had large debts. Nations like England and Spain did not want America to grow westward. The American Indians did not want American pioneers to take over their land. The states argued about borders and trade with the other states. The new national government was too weak to solve any of these problems.

James Madison, George Washington, Alexander Hamilton, and other men gathered in Philadelphia to write the Constitution. They hoped to create a stronger country that could last forever.

General George Washington had led America during the American Revolution. He said that the national government should be powerful enough to solve the nation's problems, but that most of the power should stay with the states.

The men had a hard job to do. They ordered that all the horses outside wear socks to keep down the noise on the cobblestone (rock) street. They also voted to keep what they wrote a secret until they were finished.

A New Constitution

James Madison is called the Father of the Constitution. He wrote many of the ideas for the government plan.

The new constitution said that we would have a *federal* government system. This means that we would have both national and state governments. Each state would have its own government, and there would also be one national government for all of the states.

Our national government is made up of three branches. Look at what each branch does:

• **Legislative Branch:** This branch makes the laws. It is the United States Congress. It is made up of the Senate and the House of Representatives.

• **Executive Branch:** This branch carries out the laws. The president of the United States is the head of this branch.

• **Judicial Branch:** This branch says what the laws mean. It is the Supreme Court and all of the lower courts.

The paper on which the Constitution is written has yellowed and faded, but the words are still the basis of our government today.

The Bill of Rights

Most of the men liked the new Constitution. But others worried that the government might try to take away important rights like freedom to say what they thought and the freedom to belong to any religion. The authors of the Constitution said that these rights had been given to them by their creator. Ten *amendments* were added to the Constitution. These changes to the Constitution were called the Bill of Rights.

Representatives of the People

In the United States, the people elect *representatives* to make the laws. This is like your class voting for a representative to go to a student council meeting. The student council members from all of the classes vote for certain things for the whole school.

In government, if the representatives do not make laws the people want, then the people will vote for someone else in the next election. This keeps the power in the hands of the people.

Wisconsin's Representatives in Congress

Representatives from Wisconsin and all of the fifty states go to Washington, D.C. to make laws for the whole country. Two people from Wisconsin and every other state are elected to serve in the Senate. Eight representatives from Wisconsin are elected to serve in the House of Representatives. This is because Wisconsin is divided into eight equal *districts*, or parts. One representative comes from each of the districts.

What do you think?

- Why should the state be divided into districts? Why is it good to have a representative from each district?
- If most of our representatives came from only one district, would it be fair to the voters in the other districts?

Forms of Government in the World

democracy:
    rule by the majority

monarchy:
    rule by a single person

oligarchy:
    rule by a few

A majority of the votes means more than half.

Capital Cities

Government representatives meet and make laws in the capital city.

- The capital of the United States is Washington, D.C.
- The capital of Wisconsin is Madison.

People who live in Wisconsin have to follow the rules of both the government of the United States and the government of Wisconsin.

Who Can Vote?

Who can vote for representatives? Who can vote for the president of the United States or the governor of Wisconsin? Today, anyone who is a citizen of the United States, is at least eighteen years old, and is registered (signed up to vote) can vote.

What do you think?

Do you think that eighteen year olds are responsible enough to vote for government leaders? Why or why not?

Activity

Your Representatives

Who are your representatives? Find them in the government section in the front of your phone book or on the Internet.

Newspapers, radio, and TV are great ways to find out what people want their government leaders to do about problems. Write a paragraph about one problem you hear about on the news.

Herbert Kohl (left) and Russell Feingold (right) represent Wisconsin in the U.S. Senate in 2002.

What Are Political Parties?

Any person who is a citizen can run for a government office. Usually a person is first *nominated*, or chosen to run for office, by one of the *political parties*. Political parties are groups of people who have a lot of the same ideas about how the government should run.

The Democratic Party and the Republican Party are the two main political parties in Wisconsin and in the rest of the United States. There are also other parties known as third parties. Some citizens do not belong to any party. They run for office or vote as *independents*.

A person who runs for office is a *candidate*. Candidates raise money, make posters, buy TV and radio advertising, and give speeches. At voting time, the people vote for the candidates they think will do the best job.

During elections, watch for these two animals on signs and badges. The **elephant** is the symbol for the Republicans. The **donkey** is the symbol for the Democrats.

Branches of Government

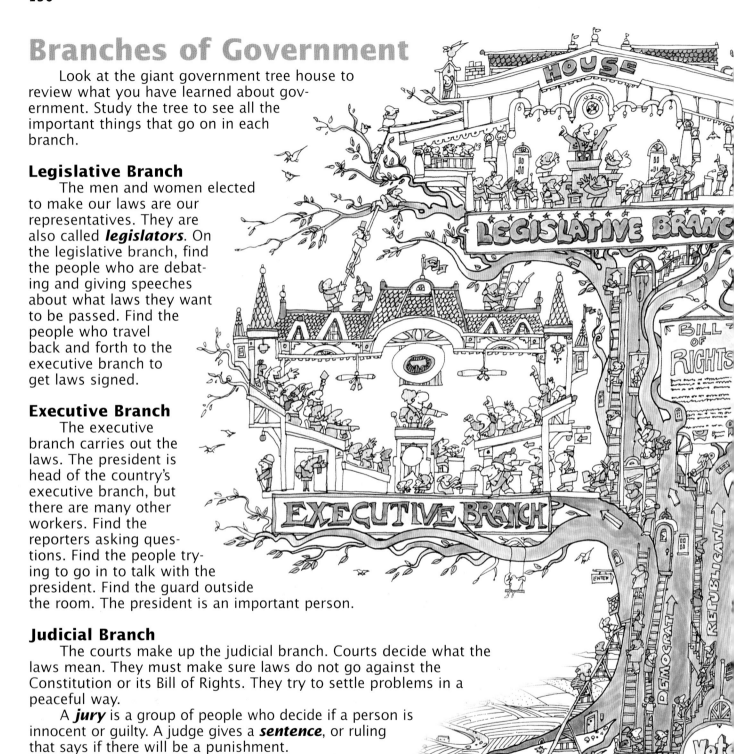

Look at the giant government tree house to review what you have learned about government. Study the tree to see all the important things that go on in each branch.

Legislative Branch

The men and women elected to make our laws are our representatives. They are also called *legislators*. On the legislative branch, find the people who are debating and giving speeches about what laws they want to be passed. Find the people who travel back and forth to the executive branch to get laws signed.

Executive Branch

The executive branch carries out the laws. The president is head of the country's executive branch, but there are many other workers. Find the reporters asking questions. Find the people trying to go in to talk with the president. Find the guard outside the room. The president is an important person.

Judicial Branch

The courts make up the judicial branch. Courts decide what the laws mean. They must make sure laws do not go against the Constitution or its Bill of Rights. They try to settle problems in a peaceful way.

A *jury* is a group of people who decide if a person is innocent or guilty. A judge gives a *sentence*, or ruling that says if there will be a punishment.

Find the judge, jury, and court reporter. The court reporter writes down everything that is said in court.

Constitution and Bill of Rights

Our government is based on our Constitution. It is the most important document in the whole United States. The Bill of Rights is part of the Constitution. It states that our government cannot make laws to take away our freedom.

Find the Constitution and Bill of Rights on the tree.

Political Parties

Political parties are groups of people who share many of the same ideas about government. Find the elephant and the donkey at the base of the tree. Do you remember which parties they stand for? Do you see another party on the tree trunk?

Voting

The most important thing to remember about our government is that its leaders represent all of us. Find the people voting for their leaders. Then find those leaders climbing up the tree to serve in one of the branches of government.

Lesson 1 Memory Master

1. Name three problems that the new national government had after the colonies declared their independence from England.
2. What three branches make up the national government?
3. People elect _____ to vote for them.

Lesson 2

State and Local Government

PEOPLE TO KNOW
Scott McCallum

PLACES TO LOCATE
Monroe

WORDS TO UNDERSTAND
bill
local
ordinance
veto

Government for Wisconsin

The fifty states of our country are all different. Each state has different problems. Each state has its own state government to solve these problems.

In the West, Arizona and Utah make laws about how water can be used. Water is very important there because they are desert states. California's government checks fruits and vegetables for insects. West Virginia makes laws about safety in its coal mines. Wisconsin makes laws about fishing in its many lakes and rivers. The government decides how many fish of each kind a person can catch.

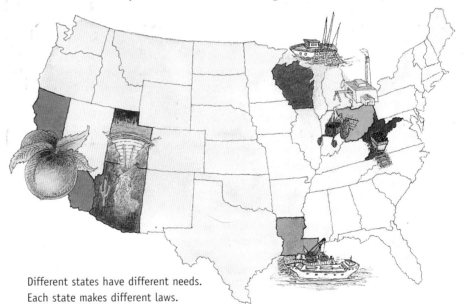

Different states have different needs.
Each state makes different laws.

State Branches of Government

Like the national government, the state government is divided into three branches. Each branch has certain duties. This keeps each branch from becoming too powerful. One branch cannot make laws without the other branch. The balance of power is a very important part of our government.

Legislative Branch

In Wisconsin, the legislature is made of the Senate and the Assembly. People from all over Wisconsin vote for their favorite representatives. Then the people can tell their representatives how they feel about problems by writing letters, sending e-mail, calling on the telephone, or talking to them at their offices. The legislature meets each year in Madison, our state capital. The legislature decides which bills will become new laws.

Wisconsin Legislature

Senate	Assembly
33	99
Senators	Representatives
—	—
four-year terms	two-year terms

Our state government offices are at the Wisconsin State Capitol Building in Madison. The capitol is a smaller version of the capitol building in Washington, D.C.

Executive Branch

The governor is the head of the state executive branch and is elected by the people of Wisconsin. Here is a list of some jobs the governor does. Which do you think are the most important?

• Sees that state laws are carried out.

• Suggests *bills* (plans for new laws) to the legislature.

• Prepares a state budget (tells how money will be spent).

• Signs bills into law or *vetoes* (says no) to them.

• Acts as the head of the state military.

• Grants pardons (forgiveness) to people found guilty of crimes.

Have you been inside the Capitol Building?

Many people help the governor in the executive branch. Some people collect tax money. Others help people get licenses to drive automobiles and run businesses. Workers in the executive branch help farmers market their products. They inspect farm animals to be sure they are healthy. Others work for our state parks. There are people who work in health and education. Your teacher has a license from the Wisconsin Department of Public Instruction, which is part of the executive branch.

Judicial Branch

The courts make up the third branch of our state government. The people of Wisconsin elect all the judges.

Courts decide who is right when people disagree about what a law means. A judge and often a jury listen to the reports of police officers. They listen to other people who were involved. The jury must decide if the person on trial is guilty or innocent. If the person is found guilty of the crime, the judge decides how the person should be punished.

In another kind of case, a person might feel that he or she has not been treated fairly. A person might ask the courts to decide who was to blame for an accident. The court will listen to both sides and then decide on a way to settle the argument.

These judges serve on the Wisconsin State Supreme Court. How many judges are there? What is their job?

Activity

You Be the Judge

A judge is a very important person. He or she must listen carefully to both sides before deciding what to do. A judge can fine people, send people to jail, or just talk to them about being good citizens. In each case, a judge uses the laws that were written by the legislators to help decide what to do.

Now it is your turn to be a judge. Read the story. Then, write how you would have these boys settle their problem.

Jason loves to use his skateboard after school. When he is finished, he always takes it inside where it will be safe. One day, his friend Matt asks to borrow it for a while. Jason agrees and tells Matt to take good care of it and to bring it back before dark.

Matt stays out late, using the skateboard. When he goes home, it is getting dark and his family is calling him in for the night. Matt lays the skateboard down on the ground and goes in. In the morning, the skateboard is gone. It has been stolen.

Jason is very upset! He thinks Matt's family should buy him a new skateboard. Matt says his family does not have enough money to buy one. He has never even had one himself. He says it was too dark to return the skateboard the night before.

Matt says he had planned to go back outside later and put the skateboard in a safe place, but he forgot. He says it was not his fault the skateboard was stolen.

Local Government

In some places in Wisconsin, farms cover the land. In other places, skyscrapers and apartment buildings are all you can see. Cities might have a very high population, with roads and sidewalks crowded with cars and people. Other places are quieter, with very few people.

Because different places have different needs, *local* governments are important. Local governments are governments close to home. County, city, and town governments are all local governments.

Local government workers in Monroe have offices in this courthouse.

Photo by John D. Ivanko

Counties and County Seats

Wisconsin is divided into seventy-two counties. Each county has a town that is the county seat.

What happens at the county seat? Judges and juries hear cases at the county courthouse. Births, deaths, and marriages are also recorded there. If your family owns property, a map of your property is kept in the county courthouse.

City Government

Another kind of local government even closer to home is city government. There are different kinds of city governments. A mayor or city manager runs a city with the help of a city council. Larger cities have larger governments than small towns.

Cities make rules about what kinds of buildings can be built in different regions of the city. They often keep houses separate from businesses. They make sure schools are in safe places. They make laws about speed limits on the roads. Cities also have city courts.

What do you think?

Can you think of city laws, sometimes called *ordinances,* that affect you? They might have to do with speed limits, crosswalks, dog licenses, garbage pick-up, buses or taxis, or rules for your park or swimming pool.
• Why do you think these rules were passed?
• Which rules do you agree with?
• Which ones would you like to change and why?

Levels of Government

The national government, state government, and local government are all different levels of government. All of the different levels of government are made up of the same three branches—legislative, executive, and judicial branches.

What level of government does the president of the United States belong to? What level of government does the mayor of your city or town work for? What level of government does the governor work under?

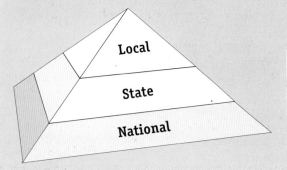

Level	Place	Head of Executive Branch
Local	County, City, Town	Mayor
State	Wisconsin	Governor
National	United States	President

Wisconsin Counties and County Seats

What county do you live in?
What town is your county seat?

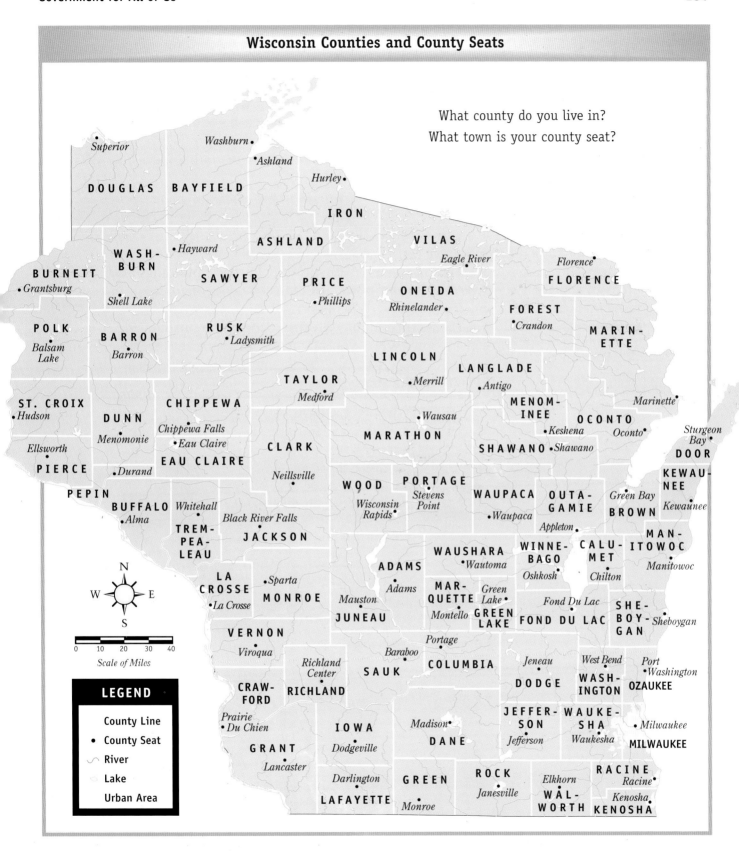

- Superior
- Washburn
- Ashland
- Hurley

DOUGLAS BAYFIELD

IRON

VILAS
- Eagle River

ASHLAND

- Florence

FLORENCE

- Hayward

WASH-
BURN

SAWYER

PRICE
- Phillips

ONEIDA
- Rhinelander

FOREST
- Crandon

MARIN-
ETTE

BURNETT
- Grantsburg

- Shell Lake

LINCOLN
- Merrill

LANGLADE
- Antigo

POLK
- Balsam
  Lake

BARRON
- Barron

RUSK
- Ladysmith

MENOM-
INEE

OCONTO

- Marinette

ST. CROIX
- Hudson

DUNN
- Menomonie

CHIPPEWA
- Chippewa Falls
- Eau Claire

TAYLOR
- Medford

- Wausau

MARATHON

- Keshena

SHAWANO
- Shawano

- Oconto

Sturgeon
Bay

DOOR

- Ellsworth

PIERCE

- Durand

EAU CLAIRE

CLARK
- Neillsville

KEWAU-
NEE

PEPIN

BUFFALO
- Alma

- Whitehall

TREM-
PEA-
LEAU

- Black River Falls

JACKSON

WOOD
- Wisconsin
  Rapids

PORTAGE
- Stevens
  Point

WAUPACA
- Waupaca

OUTA-
GAMIE
- Appleton

- Green Bay

BROWN
- Kewaunee

MAN-
ITOWOC
- Manitowoc

LA
CROSSE
- La Crosse

- Sparta

MONROE

ADAMS
- Adams

WAUSHARA
- Wautoma

WINNE-
BAGO
- Oshkosh

CALU-
MET
- Chilton

VERNON
- Viroqua

JUNEAU
- Mauston

MAR-
QUETTE
- Montello

Green
Lake

GREEN
LAKE

- Fond Du Lac

FOND DU LAC

SHE-
BOY-
GAN
- Sheboygan

CRAW-
FORD

- Prairie
  Du Chien

RICHLAND
- Richland
  Center

SAUK
- Baraboo

- Portage

COLUMBIA

- Jeneau

DODGE

- West Bend

WASH-
INGTON

- Port
  Washington

OZAUKEE

GRANT
- Lancaster

IOWA
- Dodgeville

- Madison

DANE

JEFFER-
SON
- Jefferson

WAUKE-
SHA
- Waukesha

- Milwaukee

MILWAUKEE

- Darlington

LAFAYETTE

GREEN
- Monroe

ROCK
- Janesville

- Elkhorn

WAL-
WORTH

RACINE
- Racine

- Kenosha

KENOSHA

LEGEND

— County Line
- County Seat
∿ River
◯ Lake
▨ Urban Area

N
W E
S

Scale of Miles
0 10 20 30 40

Kids! It's time to pay your taxes again! Did you know that every time you buy clothes or books, you are paying taxes that go to the government?

Other Governments

Wisconsin counties are divided into townships. Each township is six miles by six miles. Township governments are important in rural areas. They do the same things that city governments do—take care of roads and parks, issue permits, and help people solve arguments.

Another form of government is the school board. Your public school is part of a school district. Voters elect members to the board. The board collects taxes, hires teachers, and helps decide what you will learn.

Taxes Pay for Services

The Wisconsin Constitution gives the state, county, and city governments the power to collect taxes. Tax money pays for the services that governments provide.

Taxes come in many forms. People and businesses pay taxes on their income. When you buy new clothes or toys at stores, you pay

Financing the State

Where the money comes from:

Income tax

Property tax

Sales tax

License fees

Where the money goes:

Government employees

Schools

Highways

Farms

Health care

Postal service

Interest on debts

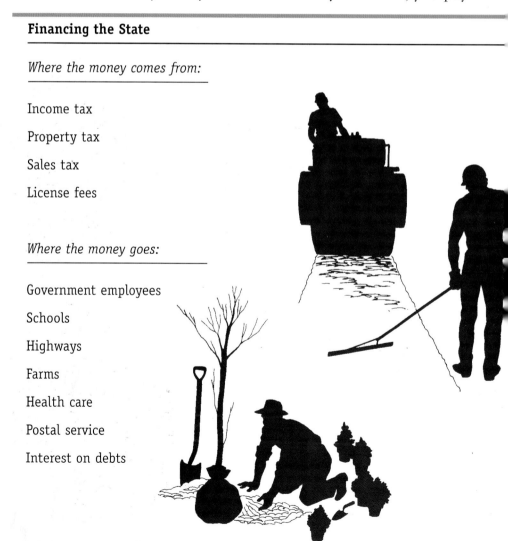

a sales tax. Our license plate fees and turnpike tolls are also a kind of tax. Each county collects taxes on land, homes, and other buildings. These are called property taxes.

What is tax money used for? Taxes pay for building and fixing local streets and for plowing snow. Taxes pay for libraries, where you can check out books. They pay for parks where you can play ball and have picnics. They pay for the policemen and firemen. Taxes sometimes pay for the fireworks you see on the Fourth of July.

Cities arrange for a clean water supply for people to use. They have your garbage picked up. Cities usually get involved in recreation, too. If you play soccer or basketball on a city team, you are using a city service. If you swim in a city pool, you are using your local government services.

One of the most important things taxes pay for is education. If you go to a public school, your school building, your books, and even your teacher are paid for with state and local tax money. If you go to a private school, your parents have to pay for most of these things.

Activity

Get Involved!

Wisconsin is only as good as its people. That means all of the people—men and women, rich and poor, young and old—must be good citizens. They need to get involved in government and help others whenever they can.

Here are some things you can do. Discuss these ideas as a class. What other things can you do? Make a list on the board.

- Obey all of your family and school rules.

- Tell the truth.

- Be polite and helpful to everyone.

- Help keep your own home and yard clean.

- Never litter.

- Never write on walls or buildings.

- Never ruin property.

- Ask adults in your family to vote.

- Tell your representatives what you want them to do (by letter or e-mail).

- Write a letter to the editor of a newspaper. Letters from kids often get published!

- Talk with adults about what is going on in government in your state and in your city.

Lesson 2 Memory Master

1. Why does each state have its own state government?
2. What three branches make up local, state, and national governments?
3. Give four examples of what taxes pay for.

What's the point?

The American colonies declared their independence from England. After fighting a war for their freedom, they set up their own government. They wrote the Constitution and Bill of Rights.

These important papers are still the basis of our government today.

The people vote for representatives. The representatives listen to the ideas of the citizens. Our representatives make laws for all of us.

We have three levels of government—national, state, and local. Each level of government is divided into three branches—legislative, executive, and judicial. Each branch has a different job.

Chapter 10 Review

1. When did the American colonies declare independence from Great Britain?

2. What important document did James Madison, George Washington, and other leaders write?

3. What are the three branches of government in the United States?

4. In the United States we elect _____ to vote for us in government meetings.

5. Who are the senators from Wisconsin today?

6. Name the two main political parties.

7. A _____ is when the governor refuses to sign a bill.

8. Who is the governor of Wisconsin?

9. A _____ or a _____ decides if a person is guilty of a crime.

10. What are some city and county services?

11. List at least three things tax money is used for.

Geography Tie-In

On a wall map in your classroom, locate Washington, D.C. (our national capital), and Madison (our state capital).

• How far do your representatives have to travel to get to Washington?

• What states might they drive through or fly over to get to Washington?

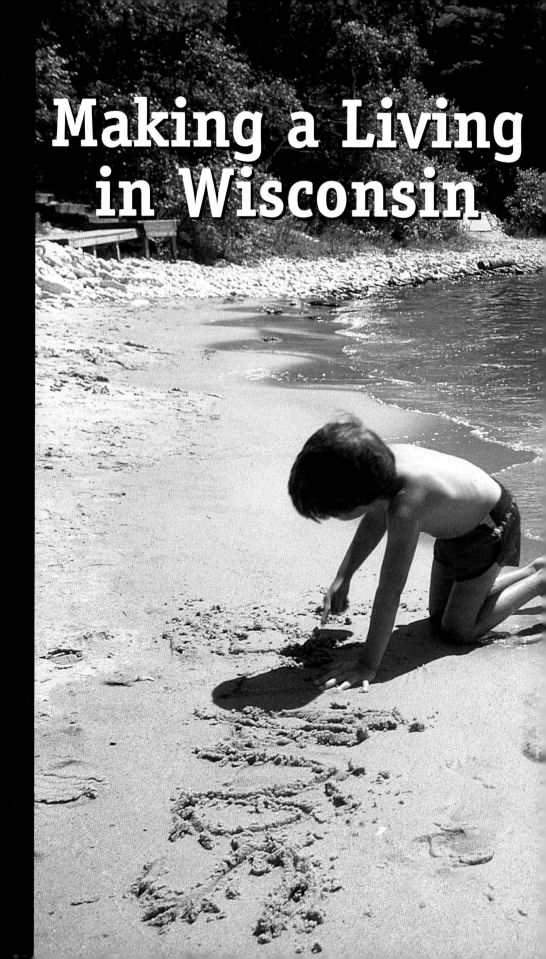

Making a Living in Wisconsin

chapter 11

WORDS TO UNDERSTAND
architect
barter
capital
capital goods
capitalism
consumer
economics
entrepreneur
free enterprise
goods
interest
labor
product
profit
rural
service
supply and demand

Many tourists visit Wisconsin to
enjoy our state's natural beauty.
These children are enjoying the beach
at Whitefish Bay on Lake Superior.
Photo by Wisconsin Division of Tourism

Needs and Wants

People have needs and wants. They need food, clothing, and shelter. They want things like cars, books, toys, and bicycles. All of these things are called *goods*, or *products*.

People also need medical care from doctors and nurses. They need education from teachers. They may want help repairing a washing machine or fixing a broken window. Teachers, doctors, and repair people provide *services*.

Economics is the study of how people get the goods and services they need and want. An economic system is a way of producing and selling goods and services.

Our Economic System

There are many different economic systems. Different countries use different systems. The United States uses a *free enterprise* system. This system is also called *capitalism*.

In a free enterprise system, anyone is free to start a business. People can make or sell whatever goods or services they want. A business owner decides what to sell and what the price will be.

A business owner usually hires employees. The owners pay the employees a wage or a salary. A wage is based on how many hours a person works. A salary is a set amount that a person is paid each month.

Business Owners and Employees

Employees expect the company to pay them fairly. They expect medical insurance and vacation pay. They expect the company to provide a clean, safe place to work.

Owners also expect things from their employees. They want their workers to come on time, work hard, and do good work. They want them to be trained for the job. They don't want workers who steal supplies or lie to customers.

Making a Profit

Business owners make money by selling goods or services. An ice cream shop sells ice cream. A dentist sells his or her services to fix your teeth.

A *profit* is the money a business earns after it pays for supplies, rent, and wages. Businesses must sell their products for more than it costs to make them.

Supply and Demand

How do business owners decide how much to charge for their products? The selling price depends on how much of a certain product there is and how badly people want it. This is called the rule of *supply and demand.*

Sometimes there is only one company that makes a certain product. If buyers want that product, they will have to pay the price the company charges.

Sometimes a toy is very popular but stores don't have many to sell. The supply is low, but the demand is high. The price is higher than if there were enough toys for everyone who wanted to buy them.

Sometimes a company makes computer games, but the game is not popular, so people don't want to buy it. The demand is low. The company has a lot of extra games on the shelf. The company might lower the price to get people to buy the games.

Often there are two companies that make the same kind of product. In this case, one of the companies might lower its price to get people to buy from it instead of from the other company.

When the supply **is low,
the** demand **is higher.
When the** supply **is high,
the** demand **is lower.**

If a store has too many basketballs, the balls might go on sale.

Work and Play

What is work? Work is something we do to earn money or to get things done. Do you have to mow the lawn, take out the trash, do the dishes, clean you room, or walk the dog to earn your allowance? If you do, you are being paid for the work you do.

Homework is also a type of work. You do your homework so you can learn new things.

What is play? Play is all the fun things we do when we are not working. We ride our bikes, go swimming, swing on the swing set, read books, watch movies, and play with toys. It is important to finish our work before we play. What do you like to do for fun?

Factors of Production

There are four things that are needed to start a business. These things are called factors of production. Let's learn what the factors of production are:

Entrepreneurship

An *entrepreneur* is a person who starts a business. The person is willing to take a risk to try to make his or her idea work.

Capital

When people use things that are already made to make something else, they are using *capital goods*. The hammer and nails a carpenter uses are capital goods. The paint, canvas, and brushes an artist uses are capital goods.

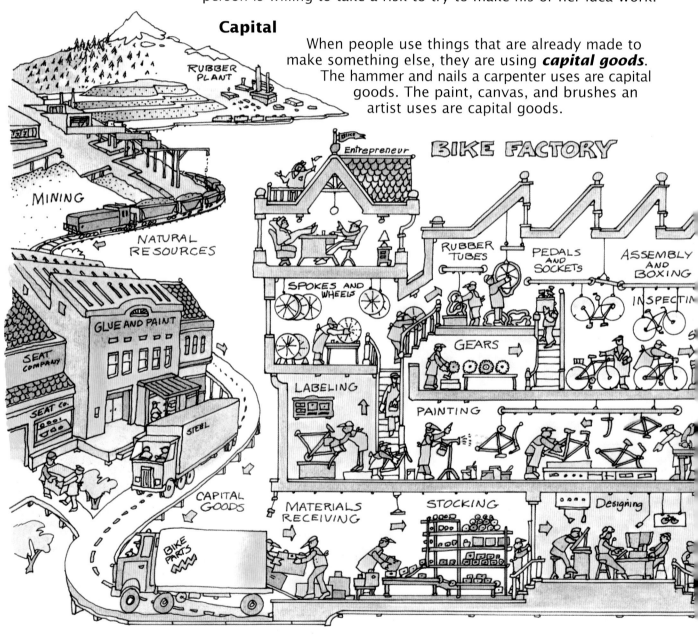

An entrepreneur also needs money to start a business. Money is also called **capital**. An entrepreneur often gets a loan from the bank. The entrepreneur must pay the loan plus **interest** back to the bank.

Land (Natural Resources)

Land means anything that is found in nature. If you are making chairs, you might use wood. The wood comes from trees that are grown on the land. If you are making cheese, you need milk. Milk comes from cows that graze on the land.

Labor

To provide goods and services, there must be **labor**. Labor is the work that people do. Carpenters, teachers, sales people, lawyers, secretaries, actors, and doctors all labor. That is how they make money.

You pay interest if you get a loan or use a credit card.

You get interest if you save money at a bank.

ME BUILDING

LOADING

BUILDING

DELIVERING

PURCHASING

BIKE PARTS

MIK'S BIKE SHOP

SALE TODAY

CONSUMER

Wisconsin Entrepreneurs

Wisconsin is the home of many businesses, industries, and entrepreneurs. Entrepreneurs work for themselves. Sometimes the whole family helps with the business. Even children help with the family business. Here are a few of Wisconsin's entrepreneurs:

William Harley and Arthur Davidson

Do you like motorcycles? Many people think they are fun to ride. One of the earliest motorcycle companies is in Wisconsin.

Today, thousands of people belong to clubs and go on weekend rides. Our former governor, Tommy Thompson, enjoys riding his motorcycle. He used to lead a ride through Wisconsin every year.

Motorcycles began as a cheap and simple means of transportation—part bicycle and part car. In 1901, William Harley and Arthur Davidson decided to find a way to take "the work out of bicycling." They were both only twenty years old. They built an engine that fit onto a bike-like frame. They made a model they called the Silent Grey Fellow. The company grew.

Harley and Davidson entered their motorcycles in races. The motorcycles could travel twenty-five miles per hour. People were very impressed. Some police departments started to buy the motorcycles. After World War I, the army also used motorcycles.

Harley-Davidson Motorcycle Company is known throughout the world. Harley-Davidson makes motorcycle engines in Milwaukee.

▲ Photo by Ray F. Hillstrom Jr.

Burmester's Grocery

In 1929, Albert Burmester decided to leave farming and go into business. He opened an ice cream parlor in Loganville. Ice cream parlors used to be popular places to go to meet friends and relax.

Soon after Burmester opened his ice cream parlor, the Great Depression began. Burmester and his wife switched from selling ice cream to selling groceries. Burmester ran the store and his wife took care of the finances. Many people could not afford to buy ice cream during the depression, but everyone had to buy groceries.

Today, Albert's son, David, runs the store. Brumester's Grocery sells ice cream along with groceries.

Albert Burmester is standing behind the ice cream counter.

▲ Photo by Karen Leichtle

John Kohler

The Kohler Company began in 1873 when John Kohler purchased the Sheboygan Union Iron and Steel Foundry. The Kohler Company produced farm equipment.

John Kohler had an idea. He heated a horse trough to 1,700 degrees. He then sprinkled enamel powder in it. The powder formed a hard white finish. He had created a bathtub. He added feet to it and began selling them.

Kohler stopped making farm equipment and began making plumbing supplies. He also came up with the idea that the sink and tub in the bathroom should match in color and style.

Today, Kohler continues to make tubs, sinks, and faucets.

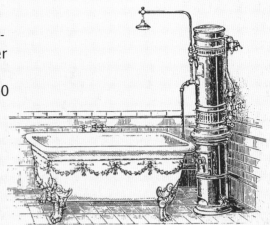

Frank Lloyd Wright

Frank Lloyd Wright was born in Richland Center. He became an **architect**. Architects understand how to design buildings that are strong enough to withstand wind, snow, and other kinds of weather. Architects also design buildings that are nice to look at.

After graduating from the University of Wisconsin, Wright started his own business that designed houses. He developed a building style called the Prairie School. This style was popular in the Midwest. Wright thought that all buildings should blend in with the land on which they are built. The low, long Prairie Style houses seemed to rise out of the flat prairies.

Wright designed many houses all over the country. One of the most famous is called Falling Waters because it is built over a waterfall. He also started a school for architects that still exists.

Wright also designed many business buildings. One of the most famous in Wisconsin is the Johnson Wax Headquarters in Racine. This building is built in a modern style that symbolizes this modern company.

Frank Lloyd Wright

Wright lived in Spring Green, in a house he designed called Taliesin. You can visit Taliesin and see Wright's work.

Consumers Buy Goods and Services

A *consumer* is a person who buys things. Anyone who spends money is a consumer. Are you a consumer? What kinds of things do you buy with your money?

Most people want to spend their money wisely. They compare prices at different stores. They make sure that what they buy is really what they want.

Advertising

Businesses use advertising to get consumers to buy their products. Advertising is on the radio, on TV, on the Internet, in newspapers and magazines, and on billboards along the freeway. You see and hear it everywhere.

Advertising is important for businesses. Remember, businesses have to make a profit. They have to sell what they produce. If consumers don't know about a product, will they buy it?

Being a wise consumer means understanding how advertising works. Do you always believe everything a commercial says?

It is hard to be a wise consumer. Sometimes you want to buy something but it costs more money than you should spend. What do you do when this happens?

Advertising

Here are some ways advertising gets people to buy:

1. **Color and excitement:** The ad is bright and colorful so people will notice it. The product seems fun and exciting.

2. **Repetition:** The ad says a word or phrase over and over.

3. **Social appeal:** The ad suggests that if people use a certain product they will be nice looking and have a lot of friends.

4. **Humor:** The ad uses humor because people remember things that are funny.

5. **Music:** The ad uses music because people remember short tunes and jingles.

Does this ad for Wild Things Sunglasses make you want to buy a pair?

What do you think?

Do you think advertisements work? Have you ever bought something because of an advertisement you saw?

Activity

Consumers Buy Goods and Services

Make a list of the things you and your family buy. Divide the list into two columns—one for goods and one for services. Do you buy more goods or more services? Do your parents buy more services than you do?

The Wisconsin Journey!

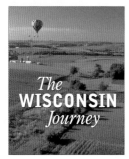

This book is a good example of how free enterprise economics works. It took the services and products of many people in different parts of the world to make this book. Here is what happened:

Wisconsin's students needed a new Wisconsin history book. The owner of a company hired people to make the book.

The authors studied Wisconsin's history. They went to libraries and read books about Wisconsin. They read the diaries of people who had lived here a long time ago. The authors typed the words on a computer.

The editors made sure the book said the right things. Another person found the photographs. A designer used a computer to arrange the words and pictures on each page. An artist drew pictures. All of these things took over a year to do.

It takes many people to make a book. How did all the people earn money?

When the book was ready to be printed, it was sent across the Pacific Ocean. The paper came from trees in Asia. Workers in Asia printed the book on huge presses. They used machines to sew the pages together and glue the covers on.

After about four months, the books were brought to America on a ship. The ship sailed to San Francisco. Then trucks brought the large boxes of books to Wisconsin.

All of the people who worked on the book had to be paid for their services. All of the machines, computers, photographs, paper, and ink cost money. Where did the money come from?

You and your friends are consumers. Your school paid for your books. The school got the money from the local government. The government got the money from taxes. The adults in your town paid the taxes. The people earned the money to pay their taxes from working at their jobs.

Economics in Early Wisconsin

Wisconsin businesses use the free enterprise system, like every state in the United States. However, a system of free enterprise did not always exist here.

American Indians did not believe in private ownership. They believed no one had the right to own land. The land and everything on it was to be shared by everyone in the tribe.

The Indians met their needs by making tools and clothes. They grew their own food. They got other goods by trading with other Indians. They had a *bartering* system.

The early settlers sold goods such as wheat, corn, and lumber. Stores opened in towns across the southern part of Wisconsin. The economy was based mostly on agriculture. Agriculture includes growing crops and raising animals.

Settlers used new farm machines that made farming easier. Some of the earliest industries, such as J.I. Case Company in Kenosha, made farm machines.

Native Americans did not have a system of land ownership.

Lumber, Wheat, and Milk

Forests once covered much of Wisconsin. But then lumber companies began to cut down the forests. The companies sold the land that had been cleared of trees to farmers. Crops grew well on the cleared land.

Wisconsin became second among the states in growing wheat. A Milwaukee newspaper bragged, "Wheat is king, and Wisconsin is the center of the empire."

Other states with better land for wheat started growing a lot of wheat. The farmers in Wisconsin needed to find something new to sell. During this time, many Germans came to Wisconsin. In Germany, they had lived on small farms that made cheese. Swiss and Dutch immigrants also knew a lot about making cheese.

Chester Hazen opened one of the state's first cheese factories at Ladoga. It replaced wheat as Wisconsin's major farm product. Many immigrants set up small cheese factories to make milk into cheese. Cheese stayed fresh longer than milk, so it could be shipped to places that were far away.

Photo by Wisconsin Division of Tourism

A reddish yellow dye called annatto is used to color some cheeses.

Cheese and Sausage Factories

Cattle, pigs, and chickens were sold for meat. The meat was made into sausage at factories and then shipped on the railroads. In Milwaukee and Madison, Germans opened butcher shops that sold meat and sausage.

Sausage was a favorite food of Germans and other Europeans. The spices in sausage helped keep the meat fresh as well as make it taste good.

Farmers sold their meat and milk to the local cheese and sausage factories. Trains took the cheese and sausage all over the country. Oscar Mayer became famous for meat and Kraft became famous for cheese. Are there cheese and sausage factories in your town?

Areas in the Midwest were growing. Chicago's growth was very important. Wisconsin products were sold in Chicago. Chicago became a major shipping center. Many railroads went in and out of Chicago. Ships stopped at Chicago's Lake Michigan port. The trains and ships took Wisconsin goods to faraway places.

Farming became more efficient. Fewer farmers were needed to produce the same amount of food. New machines helped plant and harvest crops. Many people left farms and moved to cities to find jobs.

Linking the past to the present

Today, Wisconsin is no longer the largest diary producer. That title is held by California.

Oscar Mayer

The Oscar Mayer Company grew very large. The Oscar Mayer company makes bacon, lunch meat, and hot dogs. Its main office is now in Madison.

Every summer, the special Oscar Mayer car called the Wienermobile™ tours Wisconsin and the United States. The car is shaped like a hot dog. Have you seen the Wienermobile?

Making a Living Today

The crops grown in Wisconsin have changed. Today, Wisconsin is a leader in growing crops such as cranberries and ginseng. Ginseng is a Chinese herb. Wisconsin cranberries and cheese are sold all over the world. Dairy farming and meat production are still important.

Even though farming is still important in Wisconsin, more people work in manufacturing or service jobs. The farming lifestyle has slowly been replaced by the business world of the city. Industry has become more important.

Cranberries are one of Wisconsin's major crops today.

What do you think?

Do you think there should be a return to the farming lifestyle that existed in the past? What would be the good and bad things about a more *rural* lifestyle?

Some Major Wisconsin Companies

COMPANY	PRODUCT	CITY
Allen & Bradley Machinery Company	engines and other machinery	Milwaukee
Cray Computers	computer manufacturing	Eau Claire
Figi's	mail order foods	Marshfield
J. I. Case	farm machinery	Kenosha
Johnson Wax Company	home care products	Racine
Kohler Plumbing Supply	bathroom and kitchen fixtures	Sheboygan
Kohl's Department Stores	department stores	Milwaukee
Leinenkugel	brewery	Chippewa Falls
Menards	hardware and lumber	Eau Claire
Miller	brewery	Milwaukee
Oscar Mayer Company	meat packing	Madison
Pabst	brewery	Milwaukee
Point Brewery	brewery	Stevens Point
Schlitz	brewery	Milwaukee

From the Farm to Your Table

Many Wisconsin companies make farm goods into the food products we use every day. You can enjoy a whole day of meals brought to you by the Wisconsin food companies.

Breakfast: sausages from one of many companies and milk from dairies.

Lunch: hot dogs or baloney sandwiches from Oscar Mayer.

Dinner: vegetables canned in canneries. In New Richmond, the Friendly Canning Company still cans vegetables.

Snack: cheese from many local companies.

◄ Photo by Wisconsin Division of Tourism

Transportation and Trade

Transportation of natural resources and finished products is very important for businesses. Without good transportation, many companies would go out of business.

Airports

Airports are located in large cities such as Madison, Milwaukee, Superior, and La Crosse. In addition to passengers, lots of products are transported on airplanes to all parts of the world.

The largest airport in Wisconsin is Mitchell Field in Milwaukee. The airport is named after General William "Billy" Mitchell who was from Milwaukee.

After World War I, Billy Mitchell told the navy that his airplanes could sink a battleship. At that time, the battleship was the strongest weapon made.

The navy challenged Billy Mitchell to sink several ships. At first, bombs from his planes didn't sink any ships. But he and his pilots decided that if they dropped bombs near the ships instead of on them, they could sink ships. The second day, the planes sank all the ships. The airplane soon became more important than the battleship in war.

Billy Mitchell was awarded the Medal of Honor for his bravery in World War I.

Railroads

Many companies built railroads to help move Wisconsin farm products to market and to bring goods into Wisconsin.

- The North Western and Omaha lines had the most tracks.

- The Milwaukee Road trains ran from Chicago all the way to Seattle. The route ran through Milwaukee, Columbus, the Wisconsin Dells, and La Crosse. The biggest train was called the Hiawatha Chief.

- The Soo Line ran from northern Wisconsin to St. Paul and on to Chicago.

Today, railroads are still important. A new railroad line called the Wisconsin Central was built about ten years ago. Trains carry goods and passengers from Wisconsin to Chicago.

Roads and Interstates

Roads have been important to Wisconsin since the early days of settlement. Today, major interstates have been built with tax money. Interstates link Wisconsin to the rest of the nation. I-94 runs through Milwaukee and I-39 runs through Madison.

Many people travel to and from work on interstates and highways.

Waterways

The Great Lakes provided a way for the first immigrants to come to Wisconsin. Today, the largest and most important port is Milwaukee. Superior is also an important port. Ships carry manufactured goods and farm goods on the Great Lakes to other cities.

Steamboats used to travel on many Wisconsin rivers. Today, Wisconsin rivers are not used to carry goods or passengers. But people do enjoy fishing and rafting on the rivers.

Enjoy Wisconsin!

When people visit Wisconsin from other states and countries, they might visit Old World Wisconsin in the town of Eagle, eat at a German restaurant in Milwaukee, go to an amusement park, go to a Green Bay Packers game, visit Wisconsin Dells, or go to the Lumberjack Championships in Hayward. These activities are all part of a major industry in Wisconsin called tourism.

Tourism provides jobs and money because people come to Wisconsin and spend money on transportation, lodging, food, entertainment, and recreation. What places near your town do tourists visit?

Public Services and Private Services

The government pays for the building and upkeep of the interstates. This is a public service. The government gets the money from taxes. The police department, fire department, public library, and the post office also provide public services and are paid for with taxes.

Private companies also provide services. The local video store, movie theater, and day care center provide private services. These companies make money by selling their services.

Wisconsin Dells is a seven mile stretch along the Wisconsin River. Cliffs rise 100 feet above the water.

The Green Bay Packers were named for the meat packers in Green Bay.

▶ Photo of Wisconsin Dells by Wisconsin Dells CVB
• Photo of Green Bay Packers by Wisconsin Division of Tourism

What's the point?

People have needs and wants. In order to meet their needs and wants, they produce goods and sell services. They take part in an economic system. They work to make a living so they can pay for goods and services.

Throughout our history, people have found different ways to make a living. They farmed, worked at crafts, and opened businesses. Today, people in Wisconsin farm or work in manufacturing or service jobs. How do the people in your family earn money? You and your family are part of Wisconsin's economics.

Activity

Goods and Services

Goods are things that are usually manufactured. This means they are made in factories, workshops, or even at home. Shoes, pencils, televisions, and dog collars are all goods. People make money by making and selling goods.

Services are things that people do for other people. Dentists, sales clerks, coaches, and your teacher provide services. People earn money by providing services.

Don't be fooled! Many people who provide a service also sell goods. A sales clerk, for example, provides a service by selling shoes. The shoes are goods.

On a separate piece of paper, number from one to fourteen. Write **G** for goods or **S** for services for each job listed below.

1. Works with plumbing
2. Collects the garbage
3. Teaches students
4. Manufactures paint
5. Paints pictures to sell
6. Makes engines for cars
7. Repairs cars
8. Wraps cheese in a factory
9. Delivers cheese to grocery stores
10. Makes telephones
11. Repairs telephones
12. Manufactures light bulbs
13. Sells light bulbs
14. What you would like to do when you grow up?

Plumbers install and fix water pipes.
Do they provide goods or services?

Chapter 11 Review

1. What economic system is used in the United States?

2. If you work for someone else, you are an _____ .

3. What is profit?

4. What is supply and demand?

5. What is an entrepreneur?

6. What are the four factors of production?

7. A person who buys things is called a _____ .

8. Why do companies advertise? What ways do they use to tell you about their products?

9. What ways do people in Wisconsin earn a living today?

10. What are four large industries in Wisconsin today?

11. List two types of transportation and tell why each is important to Wisconsin's businesses.

12. How do tourists help make money for Wisconsin?

Geography Tie-In

The World in Your Closet

You are an important part of the world economy. Really! You and your family are involved in world trade every day. The proof is in your closets and garage. Look around your house to see if you can find items that were made in other countries.

1. Search your closet and drawers. Read the labels on your clothes. Where were your clothes made?

2. Examine your kitchen cupboard and refrigerator. Look for labels on cans and packages. Where was the food grown or packaged?

3. Check out your garage, driveway, or parking lot. Find the names of the automobiles. Where were they made?

Where in the world do your clothes come from?

Glossary

The terms are defined according to their use in the chapters of this textbook. Each word included in the glossary appears in bold italic print the first time it occurs in the book.

abolitionist: a person who wanted to end slavery

advocate: a supporter

agriculture: farming; raising crops and animals

ally: a country that helps another country protect itself

amendment: a change or addition to the Constitution

ancestor: a relative who lived a long time before

ancient: very old

archaeologist: a scientist who studies artifacts

architect: a person who designs buildings

artifact: an object made by people who lived long ago

assassinate: to murder by sudden attack

atlatl: a tool that helped early people throw a spear

barter: to trade goods without using money

bellows: an instrument that is used to fan a fire

bill: a written idea for a new law

border state: a state located between the northern and southern states during the Civil War; they still had slaves but did not secede

boundary: the border of a country

brewery: a place where beer is made

canal: a waterway made by people

candidate: a person who runs for a political office

capital: money

capital goods: things that are already made that are used to make something else

capitalism: a system in which people, not the government, own and run the land and businesses

cargo: packages that are carried

century: a period of 100 years

charcoal: a black material made by burning wood and other materials

Christian: a person who believes in Jesus Christ and his teachings

civil rights: the rights that belong to every citizen

claim: to take something and make it one's own

climate: the weather of a place over a long time

colony: a settlement that is ruled by a country far away

communism: a system of government in which the government—not the people—owns and runs all property and businesses

concentration camp: a horrible prison camp for Germany's prisoners during World War II

Confederacy: the southern states during the Civil War

conflict: a disagreement

conifer: a tree, such as a pine and fir tree, that stays green all year

conserve: to save

consumer: someone who buys products or services

continent: very large land area with oceans on many sides

convert: to change from one belief to another

country: a land region under the control of one government

deciduous: a tree, such as a maple, oak, hickory, and poplar, that loses all its leaves in the fall

depression: a time when there are very few jobs and people are very poor

descendant: a person who is related to a certain relative

dictator: a ruler who has all of the power

district: a part of a state

domesticate: to bring a plant or animal under the control of people

drought: a period of very dry weather

economics: the study of how people get the goods and services they need and want

economy: the way people use their resources to make, see, buy, and use goods and services

effigy: a work of art made in the shape of a living thing

elevation: how high the land is above the level of the sea

empire: a land area belonging to one country

enlist: to sign up for military service

entrepreneur: a person who starts a business

equator: an imaginary circle around the center of the earth

erosion: the wearing away of land by wind and water

extinct: no longer existing

federal: government shared by both the national and state governments

free enterprise: a system where the people, not the government, own and run the businesses

genealogy: the study of a family line of descendants

generator: machines that make electricity

geography: the study of the land, water, plants, animals, and people of a place

geologist: a scientist who studies layers of rock to learn more about the past

glacial drift: dirt and rock that are brought from other places by a glacier

glacier: a large thick mass of ice built up over a long period of time

goods: products that are made, bought, and sold

governor: a leader of a state

grant: land that was given for free

habitat: the natural home of an animal

headwaters: the starting place of a river

heritage: the way of life passed down from ancestors

horrify: to fill with intense fear and shock

illegal: against the law

immigrant: a person who leaves one country to settle in another

independence: freedom from another country's control or rule

independent: a person who does not belong to a political party

Industrial Revolution: a change from making things by hand to using machines

industrialization: the change from farming and small businesses to many factories

interest: the fee charged by a bank for letting a person borrow money; the fee paid to a person for the money they put into the bank

Jesuit: a priest who belonged to the Society of Jesus and took vows of poverty and service

jury: a group of people who listen to a case and decide if a person is innocent or guilty of breaking the law

kerosene: a type of oil used in lamps

labor: the work people do

labor union: a group of workers who join together to fight for change

landform: land or body of water

latitude: the distance north or south of the equator measured along the prime meridian

lefse: a thin round flatbread made from potato flour

legislator: a person elected to make laws

local: close to home

locust: a type of insect

longitude: distance measured by degrees east or west from the prime meridian

mass production: making many things at once by machine

memorize: to learn by heart

merchant: a person who buys and sells things

migrate: to move from one region to another

mission: a place where Native Americans lived and were taught about Christianity

moraine: a large amount of dirt and rock left by a glacier

neutral: not taking either side

nomadic: traveling from place to place to find food

nominate: to name or choose as a candidate

oppression: under the control of a cruel and unjust government

oral history: spoken history

ordinance: a city law or rule

ore: rock that has minerals in it

Parliament: the group in England that makes laws

pelt: an animal's skin and fur

permanent: lasting a very long time

pioneer: one of the first people to do something

pitch: tree sap

plantation: a large farm

political party: a group of people who have a lot of the same ideas about government

portage: to carry boats and goods overland from one body of water to another

poverty: the condition of being poor

powwow: an Indian gathering with singing, dancing, and eating

prehistoric: before history was written down

prime meridian: 0° longitude line that runs through Greenwich, England

product: something that is made, bought, and sold

profit: the money a business earns after expenses are paid

Progressive: a person who wanted the government to solve social and environmental problems

prohibit: to forbid

protest: a gathering where people speak out against something

recite: to say out loud

refuge: land set aside for plants and animals

region: a place or land division that has common characteristics (landforms, weather, etc.)

representative: someone elected to make laws

representative democracy: a type of government in which the people choose representatives to vote and make laws for them

republic: a government in which the people have the power to vote and where there is usually a president

reverence: a quiet respect

revolution: a war in which people fight to replace their government with a different government

rival: one of two countries or people trying to get the same thing

rosemaling: a style of painting

rural: of the country, not the city

sapling: a young tree

sculptor: a person who makes statues

secede: to leave a country to form another country

sediment: sand, rocks, and shells that have settled in layers under water

sedimentary rock: hardened sediment

segregate: to separate by race

sentence: a judge's ruling that says how a person will be punished

service: (in economics) something done for another person for money

sewage: liquid and solid waste

shell: an object fired from a gun or cannon

smelter: a place where ore is heated to get minerals out of rock

staple: one of the main foods that make up a person's diet

strike: to refuse to work until demands are met

suffrage: the right to vote

supply and demand: (in economics) how much there is of something and how badly people want it affects the cost

surrender: to give up to the other side

temporary: something that lasts only for a while

terminal moraine: a wormlike ridge made of dirt and rock left by a glacier

timberlands: forest land

tradition: the beliefs and way of life handed down from parents to children

translator: a person who changes one language into another

treaty: a written agreement signed by two groups

tributary: a small river that flows into a larger river or body of water

Union: the northern states that tried to hold the country together during the Civil War

veteran: a person who has fought in a war

veto: to reject a government bill

voyageur: a man who carried furs to trading posts along the rivers

war bond: a government certificate that people bought that was repaid after the war

wigwam: an American Indian home made of poles overlaid with bark, grass mats, or animal hides

wilderness: land that has not been settled

Index

Credits

DRAWINGS

Burton, Jon 150-151, 166-167

Rasmussen, Gary 10 (top), 14-15, 20-21, 27 (right),
   29 (right), 32 (bottom right), 33 (bottom left),
   35, 36, 37 (bottom right), 40 (top), 41 (bottom),
   42 (top), 45, 46, 49, 64-65, 66, 73 (right),
   118 (bottom), 120 (left), 123 (bottom), 149
   (bottom), 152, 170

Remington, Frederick 50-51

MAPS by Kathleen Timmerman

PHOTOGRAPHS

Blanchette, David 32-33

Bruce Fritz Photography 154 (bottom)

Chamberlain, Lynn 28 (bottom left), 57, 71 (bottom)

Chapelle, Suzanne 43 (all)

Egeland, Debra Leichtle 87 (right)

Evans, Middleton 28 (left center)

Ford Motor Company 123 (top)

George Eastman House 119

Hillstrom, Ray F. Jr. 23 (center), 168 (top)

Ivanko, John 2-3, 6 (bottom), 9, 18-19, 22 (bottom),
   23 (left and right), 27 (bottom), 94, 111, 153
   (both), 156

Kraft Foods 174

Lange, Dorothea 134 (top)

Laura Ingalls Wilder Museum & Home 76 (top)

Leichtle, Karen 168 (bottom)

Leichtle, Kurt 84 (left), 85 (right)

Library of Congress 133 (top), 140 (left)

Lynn, John 28 (top)

Mark Hughes Postcard Collection 130

Milwaukee Journal Sentinel 128-129

National Archives 107 (left), 108 (left), 136, 138
   (left), 139, 140 (bottom)

Office of Governor Scott McCallum 154 (top)

Office of Senator Herbert Kohl 149 (left)

Office of Senator Russell Feingold 149 (right)

Oltersdorf, Jim 28 (center right), 28 (right), 29
   (bottom left)

Rutherford B. Hayes Presidential Center 41 (top)

State Historical Society of Wisconsin 53, 109
   (right), 120 (portraits), 169 (right)

Stockton, C. Noble 38 (all)

United States Holocaust Memorial Museum 138
   (bottom)

Walter, Sunny 25 (top two), 92

Wisconsin Dells CVB 177 (left)

Wisconsin Division of Tourism 6 (top), 7 (both),
   22 (top three), 24, 25 (bottom), 26 (both),
   29 (top left), 41 (center), 58 (bottom left), 71
   (top), 76 (bottom), 85 (left), 90, 103 (bottom),
   104, 144-145, 162-163, 169 (bottom), 173
   (bottom), 175, 177 (right)

Wisconsin Center for Film and Theater Research
   131 (right)

All photographs not listed are from the collection
   of Gibbs Smith, Publisher.